ENVIRONMENTAL ALCHEMY

TO GAVIN
WITH GREAT ADMIRATION
OF YOUR TALENT AND
APPRECIATION OF YOUR FRIENDSHIP.

1/09

ENVIRONMENTAL ALCHEMY: RANDALL STOUT ARCHITECTS

INTRODUCTION BY JOSEPH GIOVANNINI
ESSAYS BY RANDALL STOUT
PUBLISHED BY EDIZIONI PRESS

First published in the United States of America by Edizioni Press, Inc.
469 West 21st Street New York, New York 10011
www.edizionipress.com

ISBN: 1-931536-22-8
Library of Congress Catalogue Card Number: 2002111715
Printed in China

Design: Claudia Brandenburg, Language Arts
Editor: Sarah Palmer
Editorial Assistants: Jamie Schwartz and Aaron Seward
Cover Band Photos: Peter Hübbe

Dedicated to Roger and Gloria Stout

In a back room of Randall Stout's Culver City office, hung in a high corner modestly out of sight, there's a model of a house addition whose continuous walls and ceilings turn like an orange peel, revolving in a topological flow of form and space. Architects have long tacitly believed in the divinity of right angles, Platonic solids, and Cartesian grids, but Stout has emerged as a leader among architects performing reform theology on what has been doctrine for millennia. In a portfolio of buildings that ranges from Germany to the American South to California, Stout's irregular polyhedra, curved planes, canyonesque spaces, and warped surfaces play with and against each other in freewheeling collages of daring grace and spatial power.

> For Stout, all angles, planes, curves, and volumes are potentially divine in a canon of complexity that questions the traditional modernist equation of simplicity, regularity, and beauty. There are few formal assumptions made in his practice, and certainly not the box. Design for Stout evolves through a process of discovery that freely admits many considerations besides rote program—client interaction, energy conservation, visual metaphor, and physical and historical context. Stout allows the plurality of demands to tug the design in different directions during a pliant process that yields differentiated forms serving diverse and divergent purposes. Accepting and even building on the complex conditions of a project militates against reductive, single-issue forms. Only eight years into his own practice, Stout has already emerged with a portfolio of striking yet unforced originality.

> After graduating from the University of Tennessee, Stout worked in the Solar Design Group, within the Architectural Design Branch of the Tennessee Valley Authority, before moving to Houston to practice with Skidmore, Owings & Merrill. He then attended Rice University, and after receiving his Masters in Architecture, he went on to spend seven and a half years first as a project designer and then as a project manager in the Santa Monica office of Frank Gehry. In his tour of professional duty before opening his office, he handled many issues, from environmental concerns and construction practices, to architecture approached as art. But unlike many talents who never outgrow their charismatic mentors, Stout has established a robust voice that exceeds the synthesis of his influences. Gehry, of course, is the major father figure in this lineage, and though Stout cut his design teeth on irregularity and complexity in his office, the young architect absorbed the language and went on to his own forms of speech: there are no orange peels in Gehry's opus, and little of the sectional richness exhibited by Stout's own buildings. The image of a reclining sunbather that inspired Stout's design for a recreation center on an island on the Steinhüde Sea near Hanover, Germany, exhibits more of an affinity to Cubist abstraction than to Gehry. The lessons that Stout took from Gehry are the same as those that Gehry himself took from the artists with whom he associated early in his career: pursue the visual fascinations your own eye discovers. As Joseph Campbell would advise, follow your bliss.

> Stout did inherit the momentum of Gehry's work in Germany. The young architect, who had worked with Gehry on his Energy Forum and Innovation in Bad Oeyhausen, took on a project for a power plant for the EMR Utility Company in Minden, which Gehry declined. The client, who had developed a highly efficient application of an energy co-generation process, wanted a building that would sig-

nal innovation through progressive design. Stout responded by housing two turbines in an opposing pair of simple prismatic forms culminating in a glass and steel geyser of space. Stout celebrated the confluence of energy in this central area with a dramatic orchestration of convergent pipes.

> The Minden energy plant led to a suite of related projects in Germany that were linked by program and sensibility to a concern for the environment. Having worked with the TVA straight out of school, Stout brought an environmental expertise to ecologically driven commissions whose progressive posture encouraged typological and formal innovation. Characteristically, the architect expressed the constituent parts—dynamizing the individual forms, flaring, curving, lifting, or spinning them so they are in constant change—to create an unfolding architecture in a state of perpetual becoming.

> The German buildings are all ecologically responsible, but what makes them significant both individually and as a body of work is Stout's reinvention of industrial buildings as totally integrated environmental mechanisms with a charged emotive content. In the 19th century, the machine allowed man to think he was independent from a nature he could control, and geometrically pure forms emerged as a result of the simplifying logic of industrial production. Several of Stout's half-dozen German projects deal with the manufacture of energy, but by designing them as environmental organisms interacting with environmental forces they harness, Stout brings what had been perceived as opposing poles together in a dynamic synthesis. Moreover, to shape buildings that address many environmental issues simultaneously, he bends, deforms, and reforms the architecture, angling planes to capture the best sun, hollowing interiors to induce circulatory drafts.

> Evading geometric purity, Stout steps into Expressionist territory: the calculus of climate control and energy conservation stages the groundwork for a design liberation that leads from objective to subjective form-making. Especially in the German context, the work is illuminating. Germany was the country that first merged architecture and industry to produce functionalist architecture, forging an industrial aesthetic from an industrial ethic. But German architects, disillusioned with the machinery of destruction wielded during the war, reacted against the amorality of the machine, creating crystalline visions of cleansing purity and aspiration. Germany championed the Expressionist counterrevolution after starting the functionalist revolutions, and Stout then, in a second synthesis, reconciles both revolutions in the same buildings: he merges what became Bauhaus rationalism with the emotive capacity of Expressionism.

> Yoking irregular forms of great diversity in unusual compositions, Stout succeeds in building a warm rather than cold logic, one that embraces many more issues than simple environmental economics: he is a green architect, but not only green. Disparate forms that he keeps separate are arranged in an eruptive syntax—and the combustive energy resonates with the functional purpose of the building. Parts move as though in a process of formation and deformation.

> Stout founded his practice on the German work, but he has made the transition to American commissions with no loss of intensity. In the United States he still addresses multiple issues without forcing them into the box of a unified, reductive vision. From Germany he also carries over a strong relationship he had with industrial materials—corrugated metal, standard aluminum components, concrete, and polycarbonate sheets—that allow him to build eco-

nomically. Stout's gestural riffs free him from a need for the crutch of marble, granite, and exotic materials, and the inexpensiveness of the industrial materials helps pay for the complexities of space and form with which Stout expresses the diversity of issues contained by the buildings. The sculptural shapes usually whisk the eye away from detail, spreading attention over broad surfaces that define big volumes. His abstractions are full-bodied: the industrial palette gives the buildings a frank physicality and visual integrity that even appeals to institutional clients such as museums and universities, many of them more interested in displaying ideas than wealth.

> His designs, however, are more than the sum total of responses to programmatic and practical concerns. Stout characteristically imports an inspirational visual metaphor to his projects. Antelope Canyon near Page, Arizona, with its tall, narrow, almost wailing gorges, inspired the vaulted interior space between the volumes housing the conference center and office areas in his design for the Bückeburg Gas & Water Company. The Bünde Fire Station took its inspiration from a Flamenco performance in Spain. Stout recalls that each dancer brought an individual "charisma and persona" to the dance floor, converging in an electrifying encounter. In his resulting design, the long autonomous shapes of the vehicle halls spiral into two- and three-story structures whose ends morph into rooms with balconies, courtyards, patios, and overhangs. Visual metaphors like Flamenco and the reclining bather are strange attractors that swerve successive projects in distinctive directions.

> An avant-garde architect like Stout would hardly seem to be the first choice for a police station in Montclair, California, a bedroom community fed by freeways in the Southland's Inland Empire. But Stout does not practice architecture as a detached ideal immaculate in conception. He won over his constituency of policemen by interviewing them about their program, and he carefully built plans around their detailed needs. More a sincere listener than a smooth talker, he transcribed their concerns into a very functional parti. Unlike other architects who sculpt from the outside and often leave interior spaces underdeveloped, Stout works up his buildings from the inside. Counterintuitively, Stout shapes plans out of clear, often regular diagrams but releases the buildings into liberated sections tending to wildness. Interior spaces often soar or turn in contours similar to the canyons that inspired the central space in the Bückeburg Gas & Water Company. In Montclair, as Stout developed the plan, he conferred with city officials about tolerances for the design outside—for the public image facing the street. Having earned their trust, Stout received carte blanche, and produced a dynamic set of irregular, almost spectral forms that imply a progressive institution inside.

> The growth sector currently in Stout's office is his work for the design and planning of universities and museums. In his scheme for the Alumni and Visitors Center at the University of California, Riverside, he adapts the angular freeform design for the Steinhüde Sea recreation building, with a glass canopy that moves with great lyricism at a generous scale across the façade, creating a volumetric filigree of great fragility. He encloses the entrance halls with walls and ceilings of cellular polycarbonate, which shapes a membrane alternating between transparency and translucence.

> Stout has devised plans for the Virginia Museum of Fine Arts, the Baltimore Museum of Art, and other major institutions. The Art Museum of Western Virginia and the Advance Auto Parts IMAX Theatre in Roanoke, Virginia, constitute a highly unusual pair

of buildings whose turbulent forms—sailing, vaulting, plunging—create a remarkably beautiful, urbanistically daring gateway into the city. Their eruptive energy references the surrounding mountains of the Shenandoah Valley and cloudscapes on more interesting days: Stout has brought the mountains and clouds into Roanoke, the forest to Dunsinane. The buildings have a radiance that will affect the perception of a city they will clearly transform. The architect has taken great design pains to make these usually inaccessible free-forms practicable.

> Equally ambitious aethetically and technically— and one of the most stunning works of architecture proposed anywhere over the last decade—is the extension to the Hunter Museum in Chattanooga. Here, on a site overlooking the Tennessee River, Stout proposes a complex of shapes massed in geologically prismatic formations laced with wide ribbons of glass. Frank Lloyd Wright said an architect should never dominate a hill by building on its crest, but Stout's project is an intensification of the site, as well as an organic extension of the very stiff museum next door on the same bluff. Lyrical in its flowing movement on the outside, the tall lobbies of glass project visitors out into the view. The building augments the immediacy of the environment, unlike many designs whose framing devices distance vistas.

> The museum programs currently on the boards are more complex than the energy buildings he designed in Germany, and he continues to design the structures through a process that builds on complexity as an architectural premise. As in all his projects, Stout folds ecology, materiality, metaphor, and client input into a process that sustains differentiation and resists homogenization. His particular gift, however, is to spatialize the separate demands and to orchestrate complexity so that

it coheres through artistic tension. The spatial gift, especially his ability to erupt plans up through stacks of floors, is one that he shares with only a few other Americans, notably R.M. Schindler and Paul Rudolph. Stout works primarily by hand in models which afford him the ability to conceive his buildings spatially with greater richness than he would on paper— or even with the computer. He finally translates the sketch models into the computer with three-dimensional programs that allow him to structure the designs with a clarity convincing to contractors.

> With a new wave of institutional work, Stout is poised to embark on much larger commissions in an expanded practice. Many architects successful at small-scale work do not translate their approach to a larger scale, but Stout—especially with the recent museum projects—is demonstrating the ease with which he is making the transition. Nothing is forced: Stout is a natural talent with an established methodology. He does not work toward complexity simply for the sake of complexity, but creates environments of movement and transition, where dynamic forms seen against each other in constant parallactic shift create highly experiential environments that urge the eye on through the buildings. His strategy of admitting, then dynamizing, complexity in gestural compositions liberates him, and the program, into an arena of great design latitude.

The wisdom of these designs is that visitors do not simply consume images at a glance. These are buildings that unfold: the forms are themselves irregular, always changing relative to each other, delivering a sense of kaleidoscopic turn. The spatial canvas invites the eye and body into a roving, interactive relationship with forms that never stop. The constant in these buildings—as in life—is change. They are all, at heart, revolving, evolving orange peels.

INTRODUCTION BY JOSEPH GIOVANNINI

When I free-associate with the word "environment" I conjure up impressions that can be categorized as "built," "urban," and "natural" environments. The notion of built environment ranges from site-specific art installation to "undesigned" engineering infrastructure, including all forms of architecture from barns to important civil buildings. Within this spectrum of built intentions, my overriding interest is in innovative spatial experiences. My images of urban environment tend toward seeing large-scale patterns of connectivity, human scale, and social space. With my profound respect for the natural environment, I visualize wildlife, old growth forests, the health of our rivers and oceans, and the atmosphere. These images resonate as I simultaneously consider not only our present situation but also the projected impact on future generations.

> I am delighted that this word "environment," with its multitude of meanings, has become inextricably associated with my practice, as has the notion of "alchemy" which first came about from editor Bob Ivy and writer David Hay who, in an article in *Architectural Record*, attributed this term to the material expression in my work. Exploring combinations of common and state-of-the-art materials to create innovative solutions and evocative forms has perhaps brought out the alchemist in me, as I strive to make something magical from the everyday life that surrounds us all. Regardless of which environmental realm a particular project embodies, the following three ideologies drive my design sensibilities.

THE IMPORTANCE OF EMOTIVE PERCEPTION AND HUMAN SPIRIT

The first constant in my work is an awareness of our post-Freudian world, in which we understand the mind's perception of space as either symbolic (that which we have experienced and assigned meaning to) or affectual (that to which, as a new experience, we respond emotively). These affectual experiences elicit the type of wonder and joy that fills children's lives. Architecture has the ability to extend beyond the known and symbolic realm of architectural styles to create emotive experiences and uplift the spirit of all users and ages. The joy of providing this uplifting experience motivates my investigations into new forms and spatial qualities.

CONNECTING ARCHITECTURE TO A BROADER PERSPECTIVE

The second thread through my work is its attempt to connect to a broader perspective. My immediate interest is in relating to the world we live in, rather than the discourse of architectural history. Architecture seems more meaningful when it engages other aspects of our lives, such as art, science, landscape, and nature. Inspiration can come from observing these sources, and I frequently photograph places or objects which are not "designed," but which have strong spatial or visual qualities. Some of my photos appear on the section openers of this book. They include Antelope Canyon in northern Arizona; the underside of the Pier in Santa Monica, California; the interior of the barn I played in as a child; and some lobster traps in Portland, Maine. All of these images are examples of delightful spatial and visual experiences based on the manipulation of light, structure, and enclosure. Similarly, I often reference the work of artists and photographers and include Richard Serra, Joel Shapiro, Robert Stackhouse, and Francis Joseph Bruguiere among my prevalent influences.

> The world of science also contains an unbridled fascination for me. The Hubble telescope's first glimpses of nebula beyond our solar system and merging galaxies 300 million light years away exemplify how science provides new insight and understanding as, beyond astronomy, do the innumerable advances in computing, biotechnology, and molecular sciences. The making of architecture, from design through fabrication, should

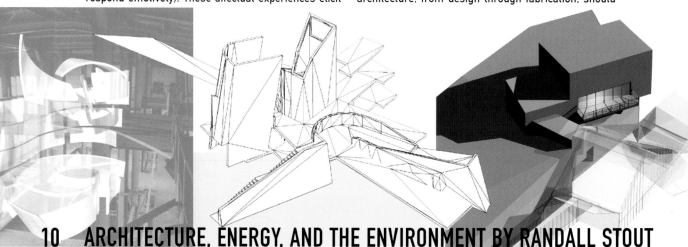

10   ARCHITECTURE, ENERGY, AND THE ENVIRONMENT BY RANDALL STOUT

simultaneously engage the breadth of contemporary life and the new technologies, materials, and automated construction methods that define our 21st century.

It is my belief that architecture can yield meaningful personal experiences and also collectively help us question, understand, and define our contemporary society. By artistically engaging current technology and social concerns, it becomes possible to view architecture, society, and culture from a new perspective. It is up to each visitor of our buildings to come away with their own understanding of what we have done. To me, this perspective jettisons prejudice and socioeconomic hierarchy, welcoming all people to a holistic enjoyment of the world in which we live.

PROCESS

> One of the most important steps in
> the process is listening.

I listen intently to clients and ask numerous questions to understand their goals and philosophy, as well as their program and functional relationships. Finding the ideal functional diagram is basic to a successful project. Therefore, my firm often generates several model studies that relate to program distribution on the site, functional adjacencies, contextual issues, and massing before the form studies are begun. Neither my formal solutions nor the design references are premeditated; rather, they are the result of a highly involved study technique that utilizes models, computers, sketches, analytic diagrams, and photography, while simultaneously engaging in an intensive dialogue and relationship with the client and the site.

> A significant part of our design process relies upon the use of models at various scales to address everything from how the building fits within the neighborhood to full-size mock-ups of construction details. This highly visual, hands-on medium facilitates client understanding and participation. During this process we collaborate fully with the client and the end-users to explore and more accurately understand their goals and attitudes. Integrating the clients and users as members of the design team results in an exciting aesthetic variety. The models often range from simple wood blocks that represent massing to refined assemblies including interiors and internal lighting to create nighttime images. The ability to solve planning and programmatic problems in relation to urban context is enhanced with this methodology. These models—despite being "process" models—serve well to build client support and community enthusiasm for projects. They also allow the engineer/consultant and contractor team to clearly visualize the project, thereby improving quality control in construction documents and clarifying bidders' understanding of the construction requirements. When possible, I photograph the models myself, as I find the camera has a distinct way of forcing the eye to realistically evaluate visual compositions from the user's position on the ground plane. This personal view allows the client to avoid misinterpretating the views of the model, (for example, as when seen only from above or from improbable angles, i.e. the helicopter view).

> Where appropriate, computer applications help clarify building geometries. While our design process often leads toward complex, unique forms, the computer helps us document rational and buildable solutions based on readily available construction systems and materials. Our databases reduce the need to interpret the design during the construction phase. In fact, one of our buildings, the Steinhüde Sea Recreational Facility, was built without conventional construction documents. Instead, it was constructed as a panelized assembly in a factory from the three-dimensional computer databases that were created at the end of the design development

phase. It was our first project for which the contractor submitted the entire building as something of a shop drawing. In the factory setting, portions of the project were uniquely and economically fabricated by computer/robotic-driven cutting and assembly devices, in a process coming to be known as "mass customization."

> As a firm, we appreciate the craft of building and frequently establish working relationships with the building tradespeople during the design process. Trades craftsmen often know better than anyone else what creative direction their materials and fabrication tools will support versus what would surpass technical or cost limitations. When they are brought in early in the work process to participate with the design team, they gain a sense of ownership and commitment to the project that greatly benefits construction. These relationships allow us to explore unique materials and systems applications while maintaining constructability and controlling costs.

> This intensive process leads to buildings that respond to our clients' needs. The clients' design aspirations, aesthetic preferences, site, program, budget, and schedule are integral to the generative forces for design. We delight in elevating all these to their fullest potential.

APPLYING ENVIRONMENTAL SOLUTIONS

My earliest training as an architect was within the unique context of a small group of architects working for a federal agency with a shared commitment to residential applications of passive and active solar energy design. The time I spent with this team, the Solar Design Group of the Tennessee Valley Authority (TVA), from 1979 to 1981, occurred during a period when energy policy was a national priority. At that time, President Carter had provided federal funding for the TVA solar research and development programs. The logic of solar energy applications combined with an understanding of fundamental design issues has remained with me throughout my career while the topic has fluctuated in political importance, frequently vanishing entirely from the client's perspective.

> Today, building energy and environmental issues are regaining interest in the public and political realms. With evidence of global warming, atmospheric dissipation, greenhouse gases, and acceptance by scientific and political communities (as demonstrated by 1999's Kyoto Accord) of the damage caused by common methods of powering, heating, and cooling buildings, we must examine the ability of building envelopes not only to minimize consumption, but also to contribute significantly as a production resource.

> As responsible participants in the building industry, our concern for the environment and the world we leave to future generations should mandate that design professionals, clients, regulatory agencies, and lending institutions commit to making buildings that maximize environmentally friendly design and technology.

> Numerous projects in this monograph utilize renewable resource technology. As I give an overview of my firm's work, I feel it is imperative to discuss energy applications and their environmental contributions. Often the public perceives energy-conscious design as an afterthought, as frequently seen in roof-mounted solar collectors treated as appliqué to conventional forms. To me, a more engaging approach allows building designs to be informed by energy concepts from their inception so that the energy applications bring their own aesthetic influence into the design mix of concerns, which includes form, space, light, shadow, and materiality. Our buildings have taken this approach with a multitude of renewable energy systems and environmentally sensitive applications including natural ventilation, daylighting, passive heat gain, gray water recovery, photovoltaic cell electricity production, solar

12

hot water collectors, co-generation, and high perform-ance glazing systems.

> The accomplishments on our overseas projects are in large measure due to the enlightened approach to energy-conscious design that exists in Germany. Firstly, the political strength of the Green Party affects design through an energy policy evidenced in each step of the building permit applications process. Secondly, German lending institutions and governmental agen-cies take the long-term view of the development process; therefore, German buildings are frequently built with more durable materials that are intended for 50- to 100-year lifecycles. This long-term view enables financial institutions to consider not only the initial capital expenditure (as usually occurs in the U.S.), but also the projected lifecycle cost savings from reduced energy consumption. Lastly, European energy and manufacturing companies have managed to avoid the patent purchase and suppression syndrome that has hindered manufacturing of solar-related products in the U.S. until recently.

> One cannot address overseas work without mention-ing the process and the people that made the work pos-sible. Overcoming language barriers and differences in construction practices can be trying for even routine projects, requiring a special degree of patience, under-standing, mutual goals, and camaraderie. This is even more the case when one is pushing the envelope with both architectural form and energy technology. I have had the good fortune to conceive projects with a wide range of bright and talented professionals. My long-term collaboration with the firm Archimedes (formerly UTEG) on multiple projects has led not only to project success but to lifetime friendships. In the beginning, communication was difficult and we frequently relied on drawing and model sketches as our universal language. With our mutual passion for ideas about architecture

and protecting the environment came a resolve to over-come "business as usual" and delve into aspects of engineering, social issues, and economic issues usually excluded from the architect's realm. With the leadership of several key individuals, we surmounted routine difficulties such as software compatibilities, multilin-gual project meetings, differences in documentation, regulatory reviews, and the permitting procedures involved in just getting projects engineered and built.

VARIOUS ENERGY APPLICATIONS
NATURAL VENTILATION
Natural ventilation methods were integrated in the Bückeburg Gas & Water Co., Steinhüde Sea Recreational Facility, Melittabad Aquatics Facility, Rehme Water Station, and Bünde Fire Station. In each, the ventilation design was tailored to the very different functions of the facilities. In Steinhüde, for example, we integrated vent slots into the façade at the intersec-tion of the wall and roof planes. Alternately, in the cases of Bückeburg, Bünde, and Rehme, operable windows were sized and placed to promote cross-room ventilation. Melittabad's large operable glazing walls create a naturally ventilated, semi-enclosed space. Each of these designs responds to the direction of prevailing breezes during the cooling season, taking advantage of windward and leeward pressure differen-tials. Where roof cross-slopes exist, the ventilation design maximizes the advantage of natural convective air paths. For high spaces and atria, we proportionally sized ventilation openings to increase the Venturi effect, flushing rising warm air from the building.
DAYLIGHTING
Through three primary techniques, we use daylighting on nearly all of our projects. The first approach utilizes well-proportioned glass height to room depth ratios

to adequately distribute daylight within a space. The second technique uses translucent wall and roof panels to admit a great deal of diffuse exterior light, simultaneously lighting the space while avoiding harsh shadows and glare. The third approach employs a particular type of photovoltaic panel: consisting of dual, clear-glazed, sealed units containing photovoltaic wafers organized in a grid with one half inch spacing. With this type of panel, the photovoltaic cell catches approximately 80 percent of the sunlight it receives while 20 percent is admitted through the glass layers to light the space. In this approach, the photovoltaic panel serves as not only energy producer but also as building envelope and light filter for daylighting.

PASSIVE SOLAR HEAT GAIN

Because most of our commercial and civic projects have no nighttime occupancy, their passive heat gain designs are specifically oriented to daytime and early evening temperature moderation. Such projects do not have the significant thermal storage mass found in residential passive solar designs where the thermal lag time is designed to warm the house in the evening/nighttime. In simple applications, such as Rehme, we maximized southern exposure and provided relatively thin thermal storage surfaces so that the radiant effect could be recovered in the early evening, while the building is still occupied but after direct solar gain has ended. Warm air returns were designed for taller spaces, allowing heated air to recirculate through the lower levels.

ACTIVE SOLAR SYSTEMS

In Bückeburg, we used active hot water collectors linked to a heat exchanger, which was in turn linked to concrete thermal walls in the atrium. Taking advantage of principles of radiant heat and thermal convection, the automated building energy management system directs heat into the atrium walls to function as a radiator during cold winter months. By reversing the system, the walls serve as a heat sink to cool the space in warm summer months.

GRAY WATER RECOVERY

Gray water recovery techniques, used in Rehme, Steinhüde, and Bückeburg, are generally accomplished by collecting rainwater from the roof and storing it for use as a non-potable water source. Occasionally, this is also accomplished with unguttered roofs that allow rainwater to flow over a hard-scape plaza to area drains, which recover the water and store it for landscape irrigation. These techniques minimize environmental damage such as soil erosion and surface run-off that might carry pollutants into nearby water sources, while also reducing demands placed on storm sewer pipe infrastructure. The system's collection method starts with the building envelope and a well-planned roof drainage system.

PHOTOVOLTAIC CELL ELECTRICITY PRODUCTION

We have used arrays of photovoltaic cell panels for electricity production on several projects including Steinhüde, Melittabad, and Bückeburg. A wide variety of panel types has been employed, including flexible panels encased in plastic in Melittabad, roof-mounted opaque panels in Bückeburg, and panels integrated with double glass skylight units in Steinhüde, where the array serves not only the building's lighting and power needs, but also stores electricity for the rechargeable electric boats at the nearby pier. (The Steinhüde project's photovoltaic system was funded by a grant from the German government after receiving the "SOLTEC 99" award for "Innovation in Energy Technology.") To the extent possible, these systems are conceived during the earliest design phases of the project to maximize both their technical integration and their aesthetic contributions.

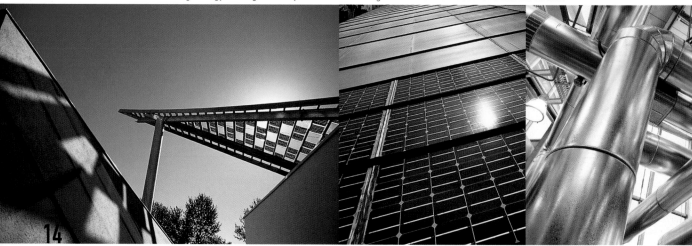

14

SOLAR HOT WATER COLLECTORS

Solar hot water collectors are used in the Steinhüde, Bückeburg, Melittabad, and Bünde projects. Some are of the conventional type: flat panel/copper tubing collector plates. A different collector type, used at Steinhüde and Bünde, utilizes glass tubes, backed with a reflective lining that concentrically focuses the maximum sun energy toward a water-filled coil at the tube's center. The greenhouse effect is at work here, trapping longer far-infrared wavelengths within the glass tube to create very high temperatures inside the collector. This system also admits daylight along the edges of the glass tubes into the space behind the collector, contributing to the project's daylighting design.

CO-GENERATION

Co-generation units of dramatically different scales have been used in three of our projects, the North Minden Power Plant, Melittabad, and Steinhüde. Behind each of these is the concept that an electricity-producing turbine's casing has cavities through which water can be circulated as a heat sink, drawing waste heat from the housing before it can dissipate into the air. The recovered heat can be used as steam for radiators or hot water for the building's water supply, among other functions. The North Minden Power Plant's turbines, sized to serve a city district, are fueled by clean-burning natural gas, as is the smaller, community-sized turbine for the Melittabad project. The location of the Steinhüde project—on an island nature preserve without connections to the city gas supply lines—led to the selection of a natural oil processed from rapeseed to fuel its co-generation micro-turbine.

HIGH PERFORMANCE GLAZING SYSTEMS

A well-insulated building envelope includes not only traditional methods of wall and roof insulation, but also the creation of thermal barriers in other building systems not normally thought to contain insulation. One such example is glazing systems. Aluminum mullions (and all metal mullions for that matter) have historically had the problem of creating thermal leaks, as the thermally conductive metal is exposed to both the interior and exterior temperature and humidity conditions. State-of-the-art glazing systems now have not only double- or triple-glazed, sealed insulating, low-e glass units, but also a thermal isolating device inside the mullion itself that insulates while maintaining the structural integrity of the mullion. Usually a dense neoprene extrusion, this device structurally interlocks the interior and exterior components of a mullion assembly and breaks the thermal bridge historically present in glazing mullions. Heat gain or loss through the metal portion of the window system is thereby greatly reduced while window "sweating" is eliminated. As glazing technologies advance, our projects are attaining higher and higher values relative to thermal envelope performance.

> The cumulative effect of the techniques mentioned here as applied in the firm's completed projects through 2002 results in an annual carbon dioxide emissions reduction of 38,900 cubic tons, compared to conventional building techniques and electricity supplied by a coal-fired power plant.

BUILT WORKS

Dynamic interplay of light with interior elements in a rural Tennessee barn.

17

AERIAL PERSPECTIVE OF TIMBERS

COGNITO FILMS, CULVER CITY, CALIFORNIA (2002) Cognito Films specializes in producing TV commercials for national brands. It needed an office that demonstrated the creativity of its business while providing the necessary functionality for the fast-paced work of producing commercials. The project consists of an interior reuse of an 11,312-square-foot (1,051-square-meter) former warehouse having an unusually high timber bowstring truss system. The interior consists of a reception area, offices, conference rooms, employee café/lounge, production pits, film editing bays, media room, and tape library. > More than anything, the client wanted something "fresh," something that neither the staff nor clients

OPPOSITE: View of stacked timbers through ramp. ABOVE: The mezzanine level staff lounge creates a new space among the original bowstring trusses.

ABOVE: Stacked timbers as viewed from the executive office area. OPPOSITE ABOVE: Inside the stacked timbers are the conference area, media room, and editing bays. OPPOSITE BELOW: These three images show how the stacked timber object guides, separates, and alters the space.

AERIAL PERSPECTIVE OF TIMBERS

would have seen before, and that would relate to the constant reinvention necessary to stay on the creative edge of advertising. This notion is apparent in the expressive assembly of timbers arranged as though under continual construction. The visual weight and randomness of the 12- by 12-foot (3.7-meter) timbers establishes a stark contrast with the apparent lightness of the more ordered bowstring trusses. > The stacked timbers form the walls of a conference room, media room, audio/video editing room, and staff workroom. They also support a mezzanine level staff lounge. Two levels of offices along the west wall serve as a backdrop, and free up the plan to allow the timbers to

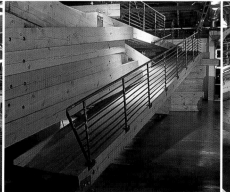

21

ABOVE LEFT: View past stacked timbers toward the mezzanine ramp and employee kitchen. ABOVE CENTER: Bolted plate connections leave timber ends free.
ABOVE RIGHT: The Client Media Room is contained within the timbers.

stand as a sculptural object. > The heavy timbers used for the project came from a local Los Angeles lumber yard and were selected from their in-stock supply of "boxed heart" Douglas fir lumber cut from reforested, new growth trees. Timber lengths range typically from 14 feet (4.3 meters) to 33 feet (ten meters), the latter length used in the inclined stack wall that borders the ramp to the mezzanine staff lounge. The timbers are held together using simple combinations of steel angles, saddles, and splice plates with 3/4-inch (two-centimeter) diameter bolts. Stacked timbers were drilled through on seven-foot (2.1-meter) centers to receive three-inch (7.6-centimeter) diameter steel pipe, and were also glued along their entire lengths. No finish was applied so as to leave the wood grain fully open to sight and touch.

22

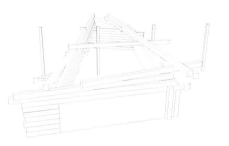

PERSPECTIVE VIEWS OF TIMBERS

1878

Images on these pages show the new stainless steel façade and entry canopies.

WESTGATE MEDIA PARK, LOS ANGELES, CALIFORNIA (2002) This renovation transforms a pair of two-story 1970s commercial office buildings, totaling 120,000 square feet (11,148 square meters), into a high-profile media complex. The client wanted to give the complex an updated new image that would complement the technology-based businesses of its tenants. The neighborhood consists of a broad mixture of building types, including taller office buildings, one-story retail spaces, and single-family residences. The two existing buildings on the site were unrelated in their form and style. The original brown wood cladding and beige painted concrete walls presented a dowdy and dated look. The new architecture added contemporary forms and materials that unified the two buildings and provided a cohesive image for the complex. The wood cladding was replaced with curved stainless steel fascias, adding five feet to the original 26-foot height. Graceful stainless steel–clad canopies serve as light shelves, reflecting natural light deeper into tenant spaces. These lower canopies also shelter the suite entries and add a unique sculptural quality at the pedestrian level. Existing concrete façades have been sandblasted to their natural state, restoring the project materials to a simple, industrially inspired combination of steel, concrete, and smooth cement.

25

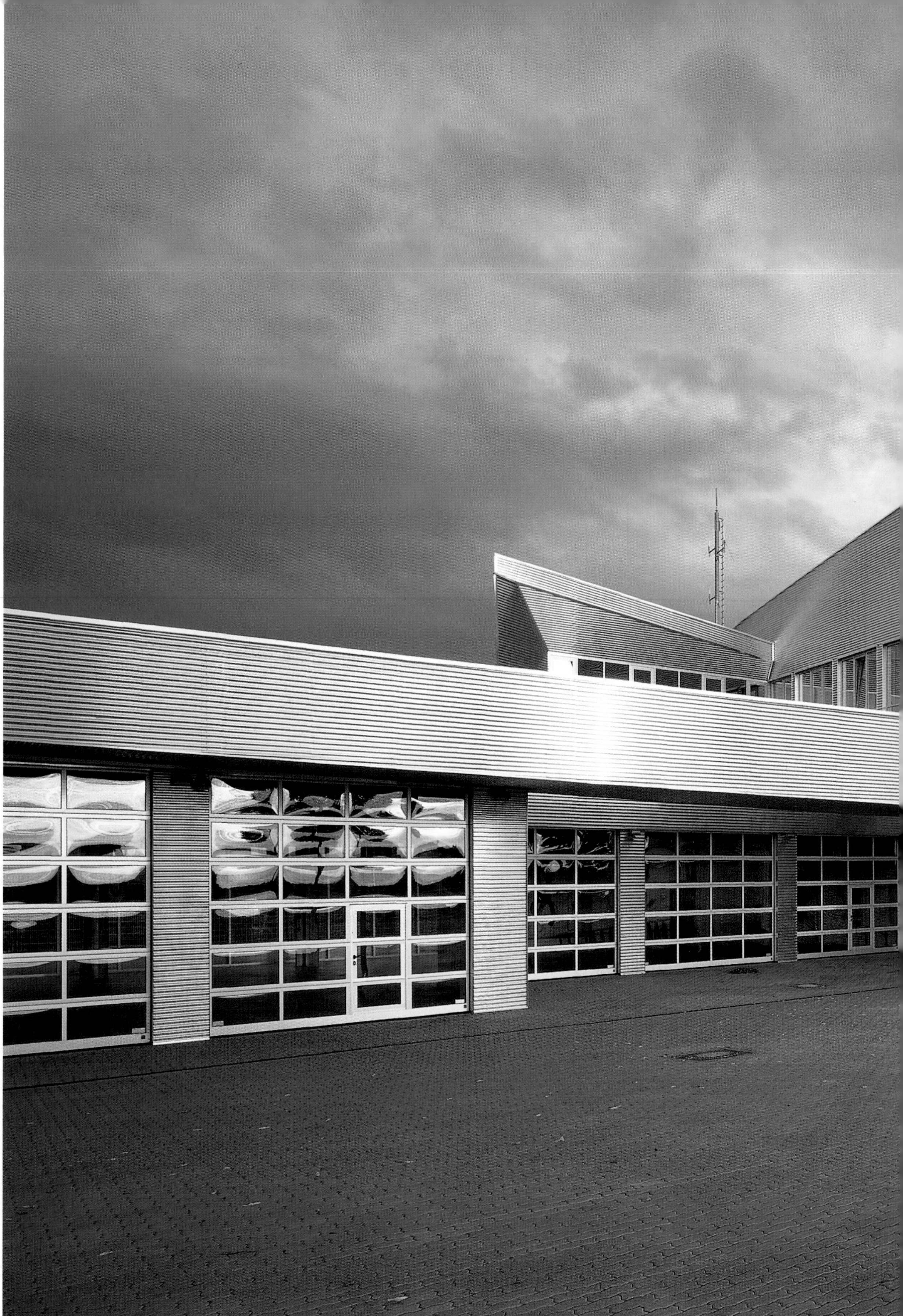

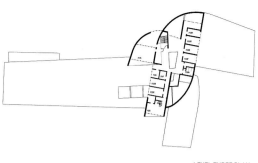

LEVEL THREE PLAN

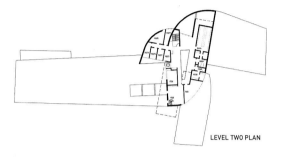

LEVEL TWO PLAN

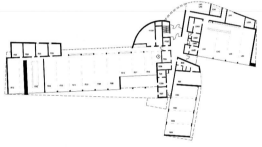

GROUND LEVEL PLAN

BÜNDE FIRE STATION, BÜNDE, GERMANY (2001) This community fire and emergency station structure spirals into interlocking forms, symbolic of the cooperation and unity among three divisions of rescue personnel. The design integrates the three financially and organizationally autonomous groups—firefighters, paramedics, and volunteer firefighters—into a facility that relies on operational unity. In emergency situations, the three organizations can now respond in a synchronized effort. Implying movement and action, the building stands as a fitting icon for both its occupants and the city. > The building fits tightly in the L-shaped site, and provides emergency vehicle access to Dunnerstrasse, a major street. Staff and visitor parking are accessible from the smaller Virchowstrasse. The fire station's size mediates between the existing urban scales of the adjacent buildings: a small kindergarten to the north and a large factory showroom to the south. Large operable glass doors on the emergency vehicle halls provide maximum visibility for safe egress, while also giving views inside the facility to passersby. > The ground level contains state-of-the-

CROSS SECTION THROUGH CAFETERIA, OFFICES, SUPPORT AREAS, AND AMBULANCE VEHICLE HALL

PREVIOUS PAGES: The glass doors of the fire station permit views into the building while also allowing emergency vehicles to coordinate activities quickly and safely.

ABOVE: Behind the volunteer fire fighting and paramedic wings (foreground) is the spiraling enclosure of shared support areas.

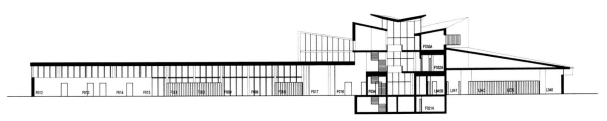

LONGITUDINAL SECTION THROUGH ATRIUM AND VEHICLE HALLS

29

art emergency facilities and related support spaces. A total of five ambulance and seven fire truck positions make this one of the largest facilities of its type in the region. Storage and repair shops for oxygen tanks, batteries, vehicle maintenance, and emergency supplies are located near the vehicles. On the same level are the commander's office and sleeping room, volunteer recreation room, and kitchen. On the second level are six sleeping rooms, a cafeteria, recreation room, and restrooms for the professional staff. Offices, training and seminar rooms, archive and copy rooms, and the command observation room are on the third level. Additional space in the basement for storage and mechanical/electrical systems brings the total building area to 35,145 square feet (3,265 square meters). > Building forms overlap to create balconies, courtyards, patios, overhangs, and other unique spaces. The strategic placement of clear glass allows visual continuity between the interior and the exterior. Exterior windows and a central atrium permit an abundant supply of natural light. South-facing roofs provide adequate surface area for the warm air pre-heat component of the heating system, as well as solar hot water collectors. > The choice of clear anodized corrugated aluminum contributes significantly to the design objectives. The directional "grain" of the corrugations emphasizes the visual movement of the spiraling forms while the aluminum's sheen complements the sparkle of the meticulously maintained fire fighting vehicles.

ABOVE RIGHT: This aerial view of the fire station and surrounding area captures the interlocking forms of the building. BELOW FAR RIGHT: Details from within the light-filled vehicle halls.

30

ABOVE: Atrium view from the third level offices and conference area. BELOW LEFT: Entry view from staff parking. BELOW RIGHT: Conference and Training Room. OPPOSITE: Atrium clerestory and day-lighting as viewed from below.

32

STEINHÜDE SEA RECREATIONAL FACILITY, STEINHÜDE, GERMANY (2000)

STEINHÜDE SEA RECREATIONAL FACILITY, STEINHÜDE. GERMANY (2000) Located off the south shore of the Steinhüde Sea in north-central Germany is the 11.4-acre (46,000-square-meter) island known as Badeinsel, connected to the mainland by bridge. Lining the mainland shore are marinas and residential structures, while the island is a nature preserve accessible for public recreation. The new 3,057-square-foot (284-square-meter) facility accommodates public services and amenities with minimal ecological impact. The four current use zones of the island are the beach, a playing field, a green area for music performances, and a nature walk with a children's play area. The recreation building houses the cafeteria, lifeguard facilities, a boathouse, storage, public toilets and shower facilities, an exhibition area, and an observation deck, while a dock for solar-powered recreation boats, an informal kiosk, and landscape revisions are also included in the new project. > The project aesthetically synthesizes components of the island's recreation and vacation culture. Stretching out as an abstract figure, the building's roof faces south to bask in the sun. Major construction materials consist of wood, translucent wall panels and windows, and metal stairs. Room locations are determined by their function, with café and lifeguard areas positioned for views of the beach and marina areas. The observation deck is 29.5 feet (nine meters) above the ground plane, allowing unobstructed views. Panoramic graphic panels identify shoreline landmarks and cross-sea views to the historically significant Wilhelmstein Island. > The landscaping emphasizes the rugged natural character of the existing vegetation. At the southern edge of the building, the curving roofline is held low so that it appears to emerge from the landscape connecting built and natural forms.

35

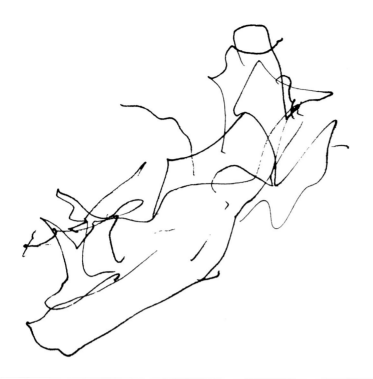

PREVIOUS PAGES: The building illumination, through the translucent wall panels, gives a lantern-like effect at night (left). Eastern approach from the beach (right).
OPPOSITE ABOVE: Gestural sketch of a reclining figure, upon whose form the building is based. OPPOSITE BELOW: Aerial view of the island's coastline, beaches, and vegetation, also visible from the building's observation deck. ABOVE LEFT: From the southwest, the building sits as a figure reclined in the landscape.
ABOVE RIGHT: The seaside north façade stretches high to gain light and views.

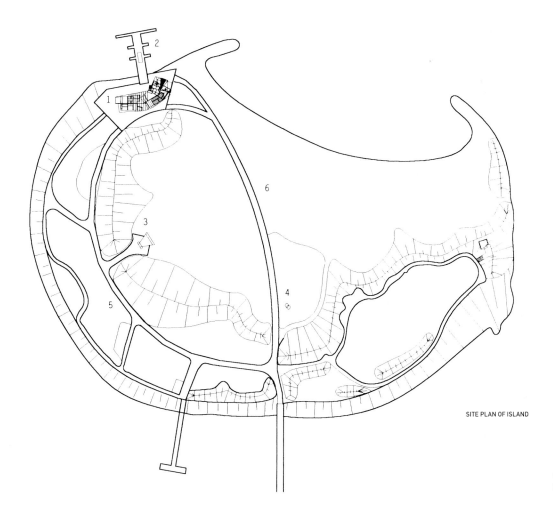

SITE PLAN OF ISLAND

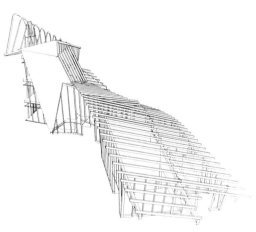

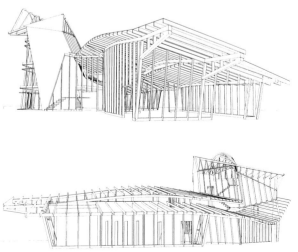

OPPOSITE ABOVE: The observation deck roof overlooks the northern shoreline of the Steinhüde Sea. OPPOSITE BELOW: 3-D computer modeling was used to communicate the structural framing directly for manufacturing. ABOVE: South-facing roofs integrate photovoltaic panels, solar hot water collectors, and translucent day-lighting panels.

Dramatic night lighting is created by a glowing, ambient light, emanating from the building as a lantern and empha-sizing the building's form. > Constructed primarily of polycarbonate panels over wood studs and joists, the building has a wood shear wall on the three-story face, composed of wood framing with anchored tongue-and-groove planks. Wood structural frame spacing matches the photovoltaic panel size, allowing for integral connection and support. > Energy self-sufficiency has been accomplished with this project. Photovoltaic panels provide power for electric boats and the building's lighting on a seasonal basis. A rapeseed oil turbine generator provides additional power for peak loads associated with the café. The project is connected to the city power grid for distribution of electrical surplus. A gray water system supplies the public and staff toilet facilities. High standards of energy conservation, including natural ventilation and building automation, reduce power consumption. > The project is on an ecologically sensitive island, inaccessible to heavy construction equipment, requiring building parts to be prefabricated off-site in manage-able panel sizes. Adjacent panels were test-fitted, also off-site, for assembly alignment, and subsequently brought by truck to the Steinhüde Sea, loaded onto barges, and floated to the island's edge. Because of the building's close proximity to the shoreline, construction crews were able to use a barge-mounted crane to place the panels on the foundation. > Through the close collaboration of architect, engineer, and utility company energy consultants. the project was recognized by the German Government with the Soltec 99 award "Innovation in Technology" and the related federal grant for the photovoltaic array used in the building.

39

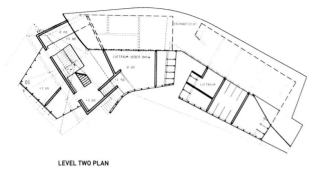

LEVEL TWO PLAN

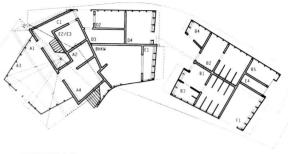

GROUND LEVEL PLAN

BELOW LEFT: Sunlight penetrating between the photovoltaic cells. BELOW RIGHT TOP: Café interior. BELOW RIGHT BOTTOM: The stairwell framing with day-lighting, as seen through translucent panels. OPPOSITE: The observation area at the building's highest point has views over the sea and horizon.

REHME WATER STATION, REHME, GERMANY (2000)

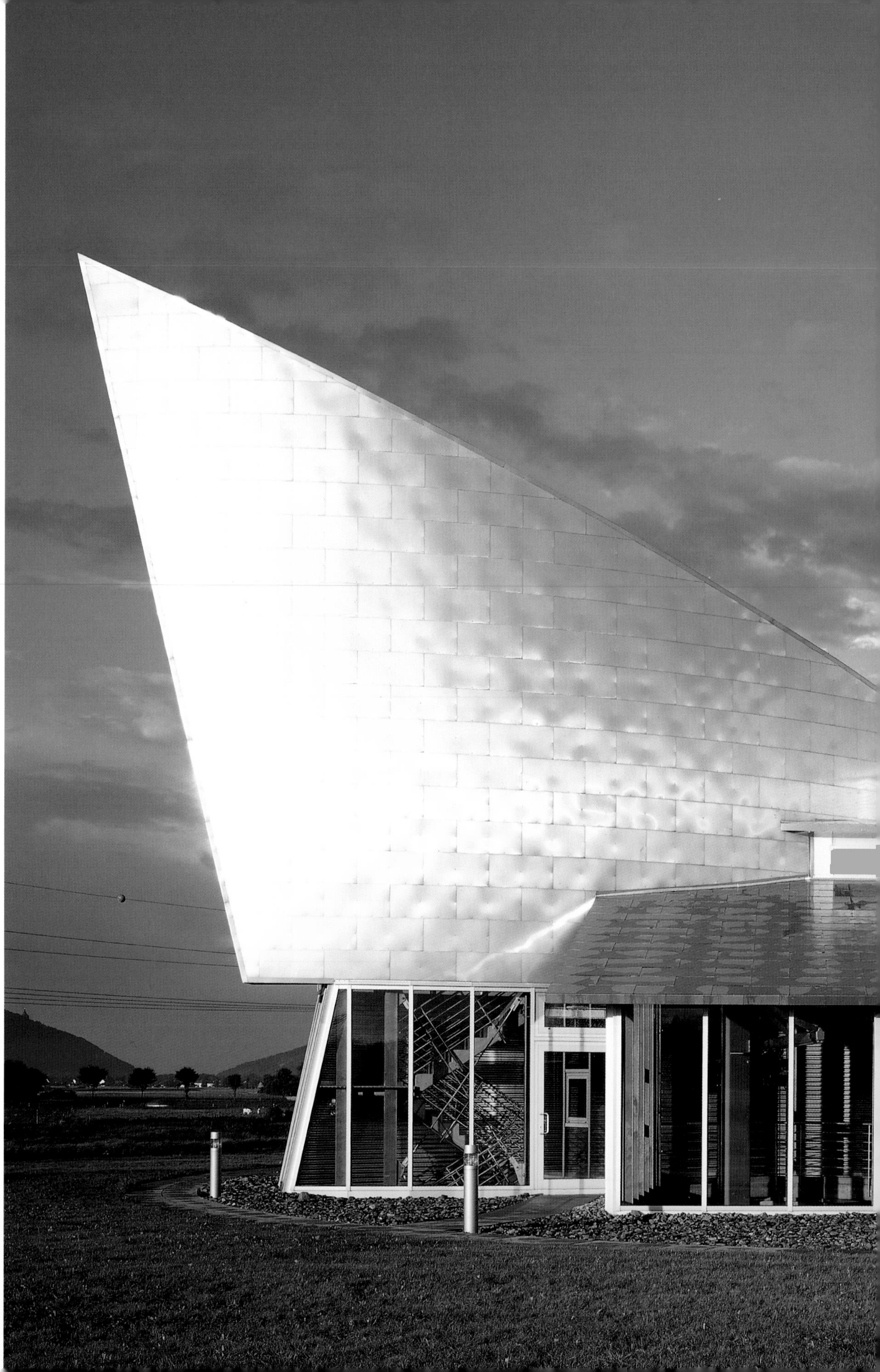

PREVIOUS PAGES: Main entry façade. ABOVE LEFT: View of the north façade from across the Were River. ABOVE RIGHT: Water storage tank and three-level office support tower. OPPOSITE: The vertical circulation space is embraced by the unfurling surface of the water storage tank.

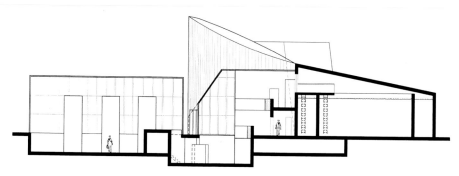

SECTION THROUGH HOLDING TANKS, PUMP ROOM, AND FUTURE WATER PURIFICATION AREA

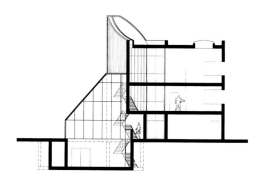

SECTION THROUGH PUMP ROOM AND OFFICE TOWER

REHME WATER STATION, REHME, GERMANY (2000) Civic water processing stations, as a building type, are often built without aesthetic considerations, as engineering customarily dominates the design process. For Rehme Water Station, a compositional arrangement of simple forms was created that responds to the engineering functions. Rendered in straightforward industrial materials such as anodized aluminum and concrete, the 8,324-square-foot (775-square-meter) project meets the low construction budget typical of this building type. Despite this budget-conscious approach, the building design has become a symbol of civic pride and beauty. The dramatic silhouette and metallic reflections as seen from the river below create an icon for an enlightened and progressive public utilities program in the municipality. > Energy efficiency was a priority. The south-facing, glassed-in wintergarten—or solarium—allows passive solar gain in the pump room during wintertime. The roof is designed to be self-ventilating for summer cooling. > The facility's site

45

OPPOSITE TOP IMAGES AND BOTTOM LEFT: Varying textures
and reflectivity of aluminum and glass combine to
enhance the building's formal expression.
BOTTOM RIGHT: Front entry.

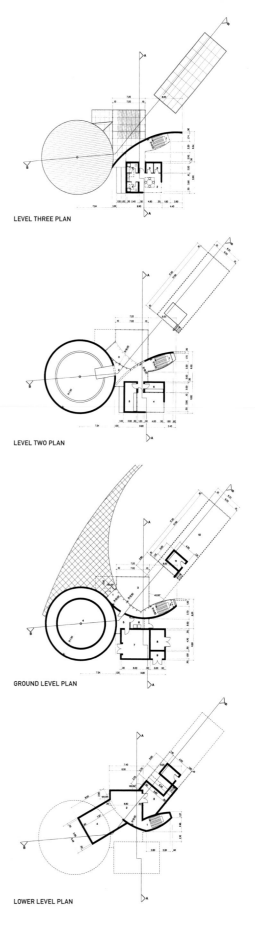

LEVEL THREE PLAN

LEVEL TWO PLAN

GROUND LEVEL PLAN

LOWER LEVEL PLAN

is a large grassy field atop an embankment that over-looks the Were River and its floodplain. The site must remain primarily undeveloped due to the location of four major aquifer wells and adjoining underground piping. Water is pumped from the aquifer into a pair of concentric holding tanks with inflow and outflow regulators, and subsequently distributed to city supply lines. Adjacent rooms are required for distribution control, record keeping, water quality monitoring, purification systems, staff amenities, and mechanical and electrical systems. A second phase filtration building is anticipated within five to ten years, due to expected deterioration of aquifer water quality. The phase two building would be located adjacent to the pump room and would circulate and filter the water before it is sent to the holding tanks. The façade seen by the river's recreational and commercial users includes a water-processing tank and three-story tower with corner windows in staff areas. > The architects saw the functional arrangement as an opportunity for a vertical composition with a spatial connection between the basement pump room, the aboveground water storage tanks, and the second level distribution control room. These three objects are rendered in aluminum and glass that vary in texture, reflectivity, and transparency. They were chosen for their low-cost, low-maintenance, and aesthetic appeal. The forms are woven together, unified by balconies and stairs. The water tank is a sliced cylinder clad in clear corrugated anodized aluminum, which peels away in opposing directions to engage the central space and contain the stairway. Connecting personnel to all floor levels, the stair penetrates the ground plane as it lifts toward the sky, implying the connection of two water sources: the underground aquifer and Northern Germany's often-present rain clouds. From the stair interior, the horizontal pattern of aluminum corrugation leads the viewer's eye toward the river and floodplain, and the scenic landscape beyond.

47

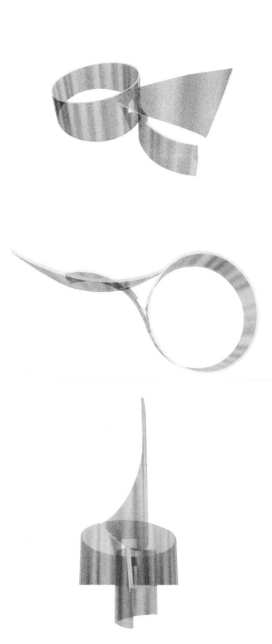

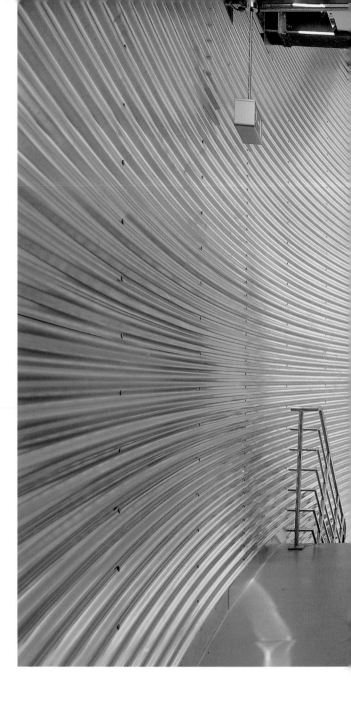

ABOVE: Computer studies of surface forms.

ABOVE RIGHT AND BELOW NEAR RIGHT:
The main circulation area provides a vertical spatial connection while incorporating day-lighting and views of the surrounding landscape and river.

BELOW, SECOND FROM RIGHT: Overlook to Pump Room.

OPPOSITE BELOW: Views from and to the stairwell.

48

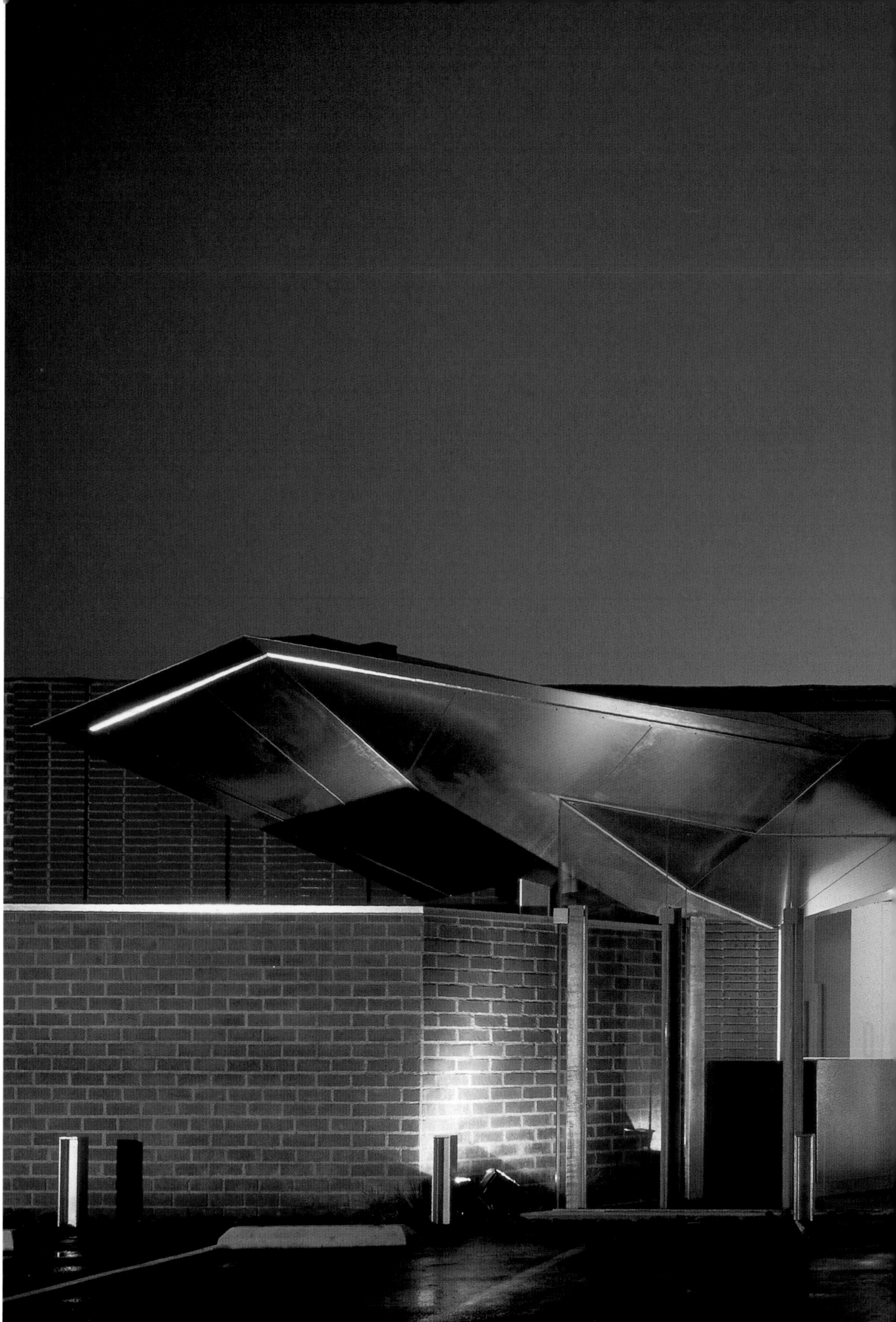

BLAIR GRAPHICS, SANTA MONICA, CALIFORNIA (1999)

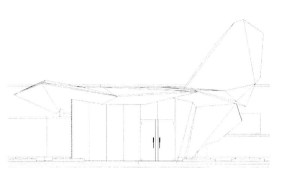
ELEVATION AT ENTRY

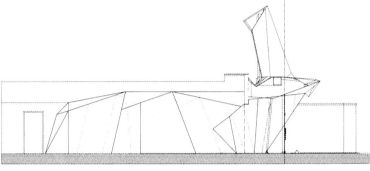
SECTION ALONG FOLDED METAL WALL

PREVIOUS PAGES: Main entry. BELOW LEFT: Entry canopy steel frame during construction. BELOW CENTER AND RIGHT: Details of entry canopy. RIGHT: Signage and interior illumination invite nighttime customers.

BLAIR GRAPHICS, SANTA MONICA, CALIFORNIA (1999) Blair Graphics is a prominent Los Angeles reprographics company that needed to renovate and expand its facility to incorporate new developments in reproduction technology. To ensure the company's future competitiveness, the design integrated a broad variety of cutting-edge machinery and technology into the existing 18,131 square feet (1,684 square meters). A new electronic digital color photo lab replaced an outdated black-and-white photo lab. Digital scanning and printing equipment replaced all of the ammonia-based diazo type printers, thereby eliminating conventional blueprinting and making Blair the first completely digital, full-service reprographics company in Los Angeles. > An expanded lobby and improved front façade greatly enhance public perception of the company. This directly correlates to the firm's technological renovations: transforming from a back-of-house service company primarily providing blueprints for off-site commercial customers, the repro service's broad new technological capabilities invite the customer inside, to participate in the digital process. In support of this corporate evolution, the architects provided an interactive, visitor-oriented facility. > In order to visually simplify the existing multicolored exterior façade, the architects added red brick walls that harmonize with the aesthetic of the original brick warehouse. This neutral, vertical façade acts as a backdrop for a dramatic folded metal entry canopy and glass

53

These images demonstrate how folded metal forms define the public circulation path through the lobby and digital proofing area.

lobby, establishing a high-tech icon for the company. With its peaked, folded forms, the façade makes a metaphorical presentation of origami paper. The illuminated canopy surfaces give the building a unique and welcoming presence. > The lobby includes a new customer waiting area, work area, and customer computer station for order placement and monitoring. The vaulted ceiling structure and new finishes give the lobby an open, modern feel. An improved staff and customer circulation zone encircles display walls that feature the company's products and services. Douglas fir–framed clear glass doors lead from the lobby to the digital customer proofing area. > The designers refurbished the staff break and lunch rooms with new cabinetry, appliances, and finishes, and designed workstations for the computer department. Code upgrades included ADA compliance and a new fire-suppression system. Building systems upgrades included new equipment and controls for mechanical and electrical components. > New materials express the technological nature of the company. Galvanized metal is used on the entry canopy, within the digital customer lounge, and throughout the public corridor, along with cast-aluminum signage. Frameless glass on the front façade further emphasizes the company's high-tech image.

54

BÜCKEBURG GAS & WATER CO., BÜCKEBURG, GERMANY (1998)
Bückeburg Gas & Water Co., a city public works division
responsible for the distribution of water and natural gas,
is located in a 17th-century castle town in Northern
Germany. The moated castle is the central hub of a radial
street pattern, which leads to civic components including
a train station. The street crossing in front of the station,
aptly named Am Bahnhof—which means, literally, "by
the station"—terminates at the project site. > Because of
the company's work with water and natural gas, the
architects strove to create a company icon that related to
the idea of "flow" in their design—the "flow" not only of
water and gas, but also of staff and visitors through

PREVIOUS PAGES: Atrium provides day-lighting and is configured for convective thermal strategy (left). Light well above the conference room (right, above). The staff entry vestibule (right, below).

OPPOSITE ABOVE: The staff entry creates a dialogue between traditional and contemporary form. OPPOSITE BELOW: Public entry from above. ABOVE: Entry façade facing Bahnhof.

LONGITUDINAL SECTION THROUGH ATRIUM

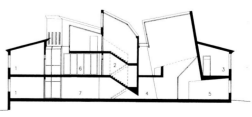

TRANSVERSE SECTION THROUGH CONFERENCE SPACE, ATRIUM, AND OFFICES

primary circulation spaces. The architects accomplished the metaphor of flow while avoiding a literal symbology of gas or water, which would be extraneous and could possibly trivialize the castle moat and other significant urban uses of water. The building's exterior needed to be subtle, substantial, and reserved—in deference to the nature of a reliable utility facing a historic district—while the interior was to be dynamic and energetic. > The resulting design was influenced by the water-sculpted canyon narrows of the Colorado Plateau, specifically Antelope Canyon in the Navajo Nation lands of Northern Arizona, where the slot canyons are created by flash flood erosion of the Navajo sandstone. The naturally formed architecture of this canyon is fluid and varies infinitely under the constantly changing natural light. Photographic compositions of the canyon inspired form studies with computer simulations and three-dimensional models. Inspired by the canyon concept, the client commissioned a three-story fresco painting installation on a lobby wall. > The project responded to its urban context by providing a front door facing Am Bahnhof and the train station. A secondary building entrance allows access from other company service buildings and the staff parking area. Between these two entries, a 2 1/2-story glass atrium serves as the project's circulation spine and the most prominent social space, improving impromptu staff communication. The atrium unifies the new and existing small office blocks that complement the scale of the adjacent residential neighborhood. Respecting the façades of existing buildings and retaining garden views, the atrium functions as an exhibit area for consumer products and services. The project materials relate to the region's golden tan limestone. > The 18,138-square-foot (1,685-square-meter) building integrates energy-efficient components throughout, including photovoltaic panels that provide a substantial amount of electricity for lighting. Additionally, solar hot water collectors supply heat to a heat exchanger, controlled by a building energy management system. From the heat exchanger, warm air is pumped into tubes buried in the concrete walls of the atrium stair, causing it to serve as a radiator for the atrium space. Atrium air warmed by the radiant heat is recirculated via ducts at the atrium's roof. The entire system can be reversed in summer months so that the thermal mass of the concrete stair walls is a heat sink, removing heat from the atrium and out of the building via the heat exchanger. Solar collectors are also used to provide domestic hot water for the building. A gray water system recycles rainwater for toilet use.

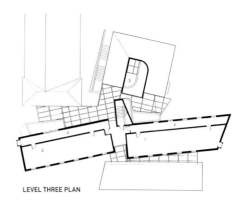

LEVEL THREE PLAN

LEVEL TWO PLAN

GROUND LEVEL PLAN

60

OPPOSITE BELOW: **Work stations with view of fresco by Susanna Ludwig.** ABOVE LEFT: **Atrium walls provide both visual and radiant energy for the atrium.** ABOVE RIGHT: **Skylight above conference room entry.** BELOW RIGHT: **Central "canyon" elements provide light and circulation.**

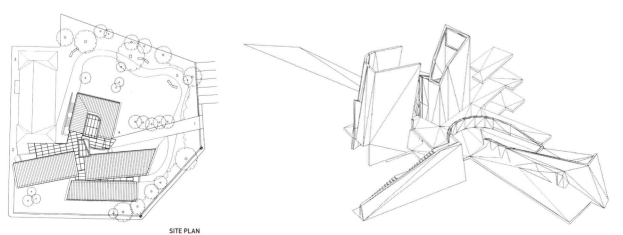

SITE PLAN

MELITTABAD AQUATICS FACILITY, MINDEN, GERMANY (1998)

PREVIOUS PAGES: Diving pool and five-meter platform enclosed by arching beams. ABOVE: A primary recreation area for this small town, the natatorium becomes a community center of sorts in warmer months. BELOW: Commercial and recreational boats on Mittleland Canal inspired the building forms. FOLLOWING PAGES: Entry tower and pool facilities.

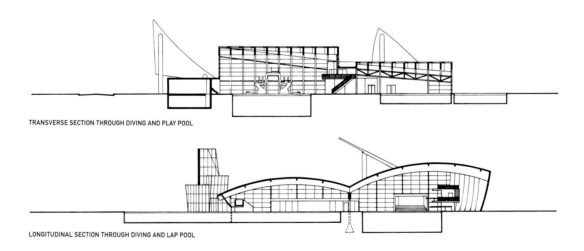

TRANSVERSE SECTION THROUGH DIVING AND PLAY POOL

LONGITUDINAL SECTION THROUGH DIVING AND LAP POOL

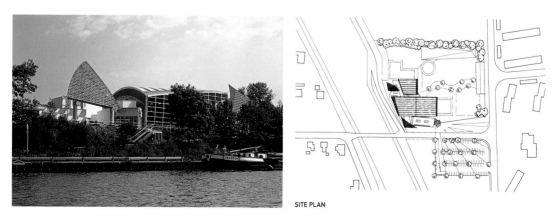

SITE PLAN

BUILT WORKS > MELITTABAD AQUATICS FACILITY

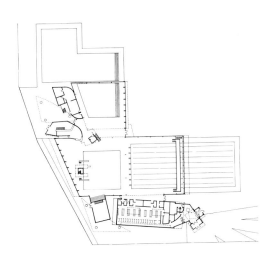

GROUND LEVEL PLAN

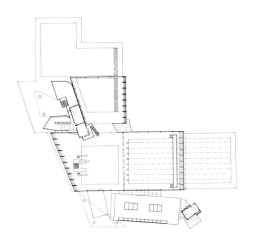

LEVEL TWO PLAN

MELITTABAD AQUATICS FACILITY, MINDEN, GERMANY (1998) The neighborhood surrounding the Melittabad Aquatics Facility consists primarily of subsidized housing blocks that are utilitarian in appearance. Most people in the neighborhood are employed by the nearby Melitta coffee filter factory for which the community is named. The natatorium, commissioned by the City of Minden, provides recreation for local children and adults whose financial constraints limit their travel and experiences. > This facility creates a sense of adventure, fantasy, and escape for children. The use of abstracted form rather than literal representation heightens individual interpretation and imagination, while the architectural vocabulary still evokes water-related objects. The entry tower, located at the northeast corner of the building as prescribed by the existing parking area, is a transparent glass beacon that glows at night like a light-house. Sail-like forms can be seen in the kinetic metal triangles that float within the tower and the photovoltaic panels, which provide electricity to the facility. Upon entry, visitors move through an opaque blue wave-shaped structure that adjoins the main pool area. The pools are enclosed by a glass and laminated-wood structure, whose asymmetrical roof arches are metaphors for marine life. > The building design integrates energy components in nearly every

65

67

aspect, including the photovoltaic panels that shade the roof decks over the café, providing approximately 80 percent of the building's electricity needs. South-oriented roofing systems integrate solar collectors that provide heated water for the pools and preheat air for the mechanical system. > After attempting to realize this project for ten years, the City of Minden succeeded with a public bond approval. The bond had a fixed limit of ten million Deutschmarks prior to the architectural proposal. As a new freestanding facility would exceed this budget limitation, the design team proposed the partial enclosure of existing pools, allowing less capital investment in pool excavation and equipment, and a greater investment in the 33,530 square feet (3,115 square meters) of pool enclosure and support spaces. This solution also provided efficient year-round use of the pools, additional green space on the site, and better use of the prime site area overlooking the canal. > Prominent exterior materials are plaster, glass, aluminum glazing frames, and standing seam metal roofs. Interior finishes include non-slip ceramic tile floors, exposed wood ceiling framing, glass walls, and gypsum board interior walls.

ABOVE: Entry tower from below. BELOW LEFT: The connective space between the angular walls of the support facilities is juxtaposed against the arching forms of the pool facilities. BELOW RIGHT: Striking visual patterns in the interior are created by up-lighting on the roof structure. OPPOSITE: The entry tower acts as a lighthouse, serving as a beacon for visitors.

PREVIOUS PAGES: Transparent façades reveal progressive technology to commuters along the Ringstrasse. ABOVE LEFT: Metal textures emphasize both linear and curving forms. ABOVE RIGHT: Corrugated aluminum on the façade captures reflections and shadows. OPPOSITE LEFT: Separation of forms between the Turbine Hall and glazed control/distribution area. OPPOSITE RIGHT: The building's configuration promotes community understanding of the renewable resource components of the power plant.

NORTH MINDEN POWER PLANT, MINDEN, GERMANY (1996) The design for North Minden Power Plant integrates advances in energy technology through the use of advanced energy concepts of co-generation (power and heat coupling), district heating, and waste heat recovery. By deploying the most modern and environmentally friendly techniques, the power plant achieves a degree of 87-percent effectiveness, more than twice that produced by a modern coal power plant. The plant's turbines produce electricity, steam, and hot water simultaneously from natural gas, annually reducing the carbon dioxide output by 35,000 tons. > The director of the regional utility company wanted the project to express a new philosophy that embraced renewable resource technology and supported the goals of the Kyoto Accord for energy production with minimal environmental impact, as endorsed by the German federal government. Added to this enlightened philosophy, he sought a design that combined social and aesthetic responsibility to improve community perception of the company before the impending deregulation of the utility. The design responds to this philosophy with a comprehensive view of broader issues, such as image, neighborhood, context, scale, and composition. The community's interest in the resulting design and content of this building led to a public arts competition after completion of construction. Three sculptures were eventually commissioned, converting the plant's front lawn into a sculpture park with pedestrian and bike pathways. Thus a utilitarian building became a source of civic pride and a cultural landmark. > Responding to the neighborhood, the building's massing mediates between the area's various building scales, which include factories, apartments, and a gas station. This community-friendliness was accomplished

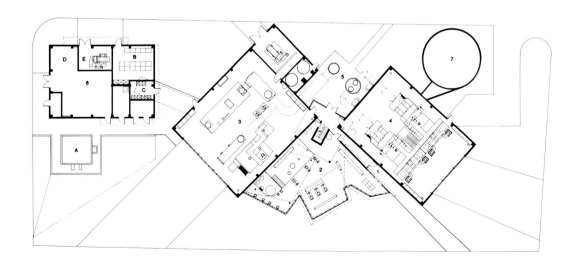

GROUND LEVEL PLAN

ABOVE LEFT: Roof view from smoke stack. ABOVE RIGHT: View inside the natural gas turbine. OPPOSITE ABOVE LEFT: Piping in the main turbine hall has accent colors to convey the range of flame temperatures within the turbine. OPPOSITE ABOVE RIGHT: Smokestacks contain heat recovery coils to minimize thermal waste. OPPOSITE BELOW: The cacophony of piping can be viewed as sculpture.

through the creation of separate volumes for the two turbine halls, the piping distribution area, the transformer vaults, and the personnel control room. The building configuration emphasizes the client's goal of creating public awareness for new energy efficient and environmentally clean power production by showcasing the energy production process. The primary turbine halls are oriented toward the highly traveled Ringstrasse, with large picture windows that reveal state-of-the-art equipment to passersby. The piping distribution zone, customarily hidden from public view, is wrapped in glass, exhibiting the engineering solution contained within. The primary building materials are honest expressions of low-cost and low-maintenance industrial buildings, combining corrugated and smooth anodized aluminum panels to create a variety of textures and light reflections. Clear glass in anodized aluminum mullions was used on all window areas, while interior materials consist of natural red clay ceramic tiles and exposed concrete with painted accent areas. > Early in the design process, an interactive relationship was established with the clients' engineering department. The architectural team tested equipment proximity and sizes against concerns of urban context, massing, and views. A synthesis of these factors led to the final plan configuration of the 16,150-square-foot (1,500-square-meter) facility. As the design and engineering progressed, forms were refined in response to specific equipment criteria, such as size, clearance, maintenance access, and piping connections. Matching the architectural enclosure to the functional requirements resulted in more clearly organized engineering diagrams and more efficient space utilization.

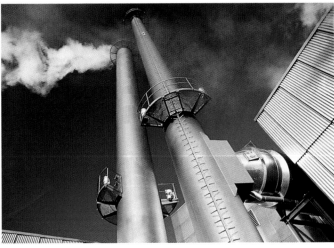

PLANNING

Found light and patterning below Santa Monica Pier.

My approach to planning, whether at the scale of individual buildings or urban districts, requires careful observation of existing patterns and sensitivity to the human impact of these patterns. Such observation results in found logics and interpretive strategies that accept heterogeneity and the fragmentation of contemporary cities. This allows design tactics that extrapolate essential qualities for future growth patterns with flexibility and fluidity. Such planning, which I refer to as "extrapolative planning," does not superimpose foreign concepts, but instead seeks to strengthen inherent values.

PATTERNS—HOW SOLUTIONS ARE FOUND

True insight regarding patterns of scale, density, orientation, pedestrian circulation, and vehicular circulation often requires rigorous study using figure-ground diagrams, statistical data, and analytic abstractions of existing patterns. Conversely, insight into the physical parameters of a place—such as its materials, form, and aesthetic—demands the more intuitive kind of acute observation that is sometimes discovered by free-associative thinking, and sometimes by simply noticing and caring about the commonplace details. In retrospect, I realize that I have arrived at this planning process through career-long studies of many important and diverse authors. Three in particular have had a lasting impact on my thinking and work: environmental planner Ian McHarg, social anthropologist Edward T. Hall, and conceptual writer Italo Calvino.

> McHarg's overlay mapping techniques of environmental conditions, born out of stewardship for nature, has greatly influenced my attitude toward analytic methods and site-evaluation techniques. He writes, in *Design With Nature*:

> Our eyes do not divide us from the world, but unite us with it. Let this be known to be true. Let us then abandon the simplicity of separation and give unity its due. Let us abandon the self-mutilation, which has been our way and give expression to the potential harmony of man-nature. The world is abundant, we require only a deference born of understanding to fulfill man's promise. Man is that uniquely conscious creature who can perceive and express. He must become the steward of the biosphere. To do this he must design with nature.

> Hall's understanding of the social and psychological response to environment, as conveyed in his trio of brilliant books *The Silent Language*, *The Hidden Dimension*, and *Beyond Culture*, has greatly heightened my awareness of the many social aspects of planning, as in *An Anthropology of Everyday Life*:

> When it comes to philosophy, all of us inhabit at least two worlds: the world of explicit statements—an outgrowth of scholasticism, learned in schools, which makes up the corpus of what is thought to be our "cultural heritage"—and the ever evolving unconscious world of our everyday behavior which guides all informal activities of daily life. The latter is so much a part of us that, like culture, it is not thought of as anything special, but simply the way we are....[I]t is my emphasis on the details of everyday life over theory, or even policy, that distinguishes my work....It is the details of the rules underlying common behavior that govern the world.

> Calvino's conceptual description of cities sets a high standard for memorable place-making in buildings and urban environments. His inimitable perception of places visited frees the mind from a singular way of thinking, allowing pluralistic meaning, as well as the coexistence of fantasy and reality. From Calvino's *Invisible Cities*:

> Now I shall tell you of the city of Zenobia, which is wonderful in this fashion: though set on dry terrain it stands on high pilings, and the houses are bamboo and zinc, with many platforms and balconies placed

EXTRAPOLATIVE PLANNING BY RANDALL STOUT

on stilts at various heights, crossing one another, linked by ladders and hanging sidewalks, surmounted by cone-roofed belvederes, barrels storing water, weather vanes, jutting pulleys, and fish poles, and cranes. No one remembers what need or command or desire drove Zenobia's founders to give their city this form, and so there is no telling whether it was satisfied by the city we see today, which has perhaps grown through successive superimpositions from the first, now undecipherable plan. But what is certain is that if you ask an inhabitant of Zenobia to describe his vision of a happy life, it is always a city like Zenobia that he imagines, with its pilings and its suspended stairways, a Zenobia perhaps quite different, a-flutter with banners and ribbons, but always derived by combining elements of that first model. This said, it is pointless to decide whether Zenobia is to be classified among happy cities or among the unhappy. It makes no sense to divide cities into these two species, but rather into another two: those that through the years and the changes continue to give form to their desires, and those in which desires either erase the city or are erased by it.

> In its basic form, the extrapolative plan presumes that, in existing settings, economic factors and technical realities have established an infrastructure of monetary value and social familiarity. This presumption also acknowledges the collective memory of a community, while avoiding homogeneity, which robs a place of its response to its particular environment and culture. Extrapolative planning is not about aesthetic makeover, or stylistic change, or creating order from chaos for the sake of order. It is also not intrinsically about symmetry or hierarchy or other traditional planning devices. Instead, it is about bringing clarity of thought and guidance to emphasize and give presence to what is unique

and essential to a place. This type of planning, sensitive to existing conditions, does not imply modest or timid plans, but rather it generates appropriate solutions, founded on strong concepts, that maximize the potential for architecture and public space. It aspires ambitiously and optimistically, but not in a utopian fashion.

BUILDING PATTERNS AND EXTRAPOLATIONS

Coherent circulation patterns are crucial to the operational efficiency and enjoyment of individual buildings or multi-building complexes. In our museum planning work, we have come to understand that gallery circulation, key to the visitor's experience, is often a shortcoming of museums that have grown incrementally over many years. A distinct physical relationship exists between primary circulation and galleries, suggesting the modulation of natural light, spatial volume, and finishes. The museum projects in the following section show several existing primary circulation patterns, many of which contain dead-ends, cul-de-sacs, and inflexible gallery sequences, often in T- or L-shaped plans. The museums most beloved by visitors, curators, and museum administrators combine clear circulation with a variety of sequential choices. Of course, to be completely enjoyable, the spaces themselves must also be well designed in detail, with places for repose, variously sized spaces that speak to the intimacy or grandeur of the art on display, and excellent lighting and exhibit interpretation, among other parameters. Here, our proposals for the illustrated spaces are shown in conjunction with the existing diagrams to clarify the proposed interventions.

> Several of our museum proposals, including the Virginia Museum of Fine Arts (VMFA), Baltimore Museum of Art (BMA), Marion Koogler McNay Art Museum (McNay), Seattle Art Museum (SAM), and North Carolina Museum of Art (NCMA), are typified by the creation of "loops" to improve visitor orientation. This feature pro-

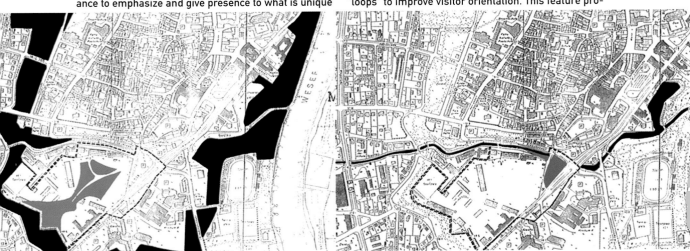

Figure-ground diagrams from Simeonsplatz.

vides spatial hierarchy relative to undifferentiated galleries, as well as sequence choice for viewing the collection. These "loops" are not neutral, homogeneous spaces; instead they consist of both path and node. The path emphasizes movement and the prospect of accessing galleries. The node conveys a sense of place, providing a locus for respite, tour discussions, opening presentations, dissemination of gallery content, etc. Both path and node are hierarchically separated from galleries for wayfinding. This is done through the use of natural light, higher ceiling volumes, and finish materials. Although the diagrams appear rather symmetrical due to the existing facilities and site limitations, this diagrammatic symmetry does not demand architectural symmetry within. Rather, the spaces diagrammed should be driven by functional and perceptual issues, and are open to a variety of architectural expressions, so long as the design maintains the sense of flow among spaces.

> Many similar problems exist in museum service areas, which have also grown incrementally. Disjointed departments lack connection to one another, as well as convenient access to closely related or shared art support spaces. Circulation that does not adequately separate art and non-art traffic can jeopardize art in transit while also adding significant operational and staff costs through inefficient communication and movement. Our projects seek to bring together related departments by functionality, rather than by administrative organization. With spatial organization comes the opportunity to provide clear and autonomous paths for the various museum services, as exemplified in BMA, VMFA, McNay, and Rhode Island School of Design Museum of Art (RISD).

URBAN PATTERNS AND EXTRAPOLATIONS

We are now well aware of the dynamic qualities of urban conditions as suggested by Alan Colquhoun in his *Essays in Architectural Criticism*, where he identified the 1960s as a time when "[t]he city was no longer thought to consist of individual buildings but conceived as a continuous and growing structure." Today, physical, social, political, and economic issues define complex urban patterns. These issues engage transportation, utility infrastructure, private space, and public domain to create an enormous challenge for planners. One of the keys in the evolutionary progress of an urban area is in determining the appropriate scale of streets, buildings, and open spaces. Contemporary cities exhibit a wide range of scales, from the tightly grained environment of independent entrepreneurs to the large grained and often generic environment of corporate America. Controlled environments such as themed parks, entertainment, and retail, although perhaps appropriately scaled, provide only a simulated utopian experience. Such solutions result in an insular setting devoid of the more complex and authentic social and economic issues present in our society. Our extrapolative process clarifies issues of scale and urban authenticity and also allows a broader cultural role for architecture as it helps interpret and redefine our society.

> One of my early urban design projects was for an office/retail district on the freeway periphery of Houston, Texas. There I discovered that the existing street scale matched very closely with the street spacing at Houston's Intercontinental Airport and was exponentially out of scale with the 300-foot-long pedestrian-oriented city blocks downtown. When the city of Houston METRO (Metropolitan Transit Authority of Harris County, Texas) proposed adding light rail to the neighborhood, conventional wisdom implied aligning it with Post Oak Boulevard and adding traditional street furniture and landscaping in an attempt to create a pedestrian environment. I sensed that this would be unsuccessful because there was no other reason for pedestrians to be on the street. Shopping and offices were set back across private office park lawns and retail surface parking lots. The

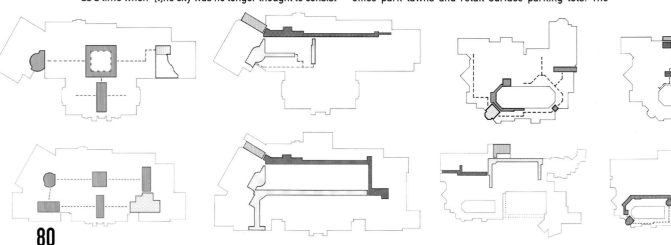

EXTRAPOLATIVE PLANNING BY RANDALL STOUT

density of light rail pedestrian traffic could not justify restructuring the immense investment in existing facilities. My independent vehicular and pedestrian movement studies revealed that maximum pedestrian density existed between the parking structures and the office building destinations. I addressed the existing path of travel by inserting the light rail into the existing parking structure system, thereby intensifying the momentum of pedestrian activity while crafting a "place" out of the transition between car, rail, and business or retail destination. The specific design of this place was then structured to accept ancillary retail, convenience shopping, and vendor stations for commuters. This solution—at first glance a radical idea—is actually more authentic to the location, not forcing itself onto the district while solving the many issues confronting the transportation authorities, as well as local business and property owners.

> A different set of factors arises on the rare occasion that a large tract of land, surrounded by or significantly bordered by urban conditions, becomes available for development. This was the case in the City of Minden, Germany, when Simeonsplatz was decommissioned as a military site and turned over to the city. The site had been used by the Prussian Army and had recently been abandoned by the British as a post–World War II outpost. Our firm participated in an invited and commissioned competition to create a balanced master plan for the entire district, and to design the phase one cinema buildings. In my approach to the project, I searched for connections within the existing urban fabric. I wanted to extrapolate naturally occurring and longstanding neighboring components, weaving them into and through the new site. This would allow the plan to unify and benefit surrounding neighborhoods while simultaneously creating a unique new public space. The many figure-ground drawings generated by our team provided the city representatives with an analytic view of Minden that

had not been previously understood. This new view gave a fresh and clear understanding of the existing physical components, which were the foundation of the "gateways" concept in our master plan.

> Perhaps the rarest of all planning projects is the creation of a new town in relative isolation of an existing population. This sort of project challenges the status quo by starting with a clean slate in the reality of the 21st century, without any of the infrastructure associated with previous centuries of incremental growth. It questions the contemporary validity of historic patterning derived from trade routes (such as Italian hill towns like Siena), or from military access routes (as in Parisian boulevards), and even questions the validity of the neutral Cartesian grid. Faced with these challenges and questions, my focus turns to the search for essential qualities relating to the purpose of a place, its technological condition, and its physical environment. This search helps me identify and accommodate geometrically defined responses to the analytic or metaphoric representation of the city's origin, using site features and natural resources. Once understood, this information allows the crafting of the new city in the *idea* of Siena and Paris (formed from real needs, activities, and response to place), rather than literally replicating the formal qualities of such places. It is this notion of intrinsic similarity which interests me, rather than imposed physical similarities. An example of one such new town solution comes in the form of a new scientific community planned for the Superconducting Supercollider (SSC) particle accelerator research project proposed in 1987 under the Reagan Administration. The project responds to its scientific nature, the needs of a diverse and self-contained community, as well as solar energy and environmental planning. The resulting urban/suburban forms shown in this project (see Supercollider City) respond to the unique needs of this scientific town and its place in time.

Analytic circulation diagrams from RSA's museum planning projects.

MUSEUM
PLANNING

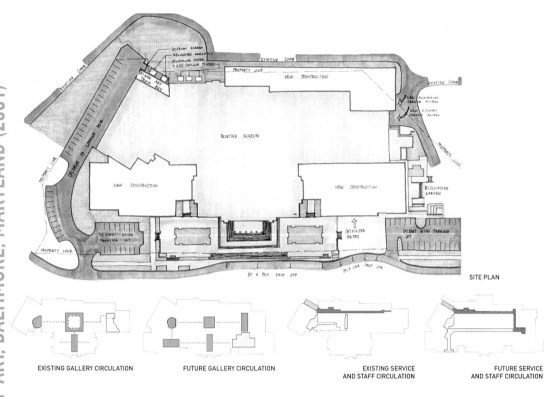

SITE PLAN

EXISTING GALLERY CIRCULATION

FUTURE GALLERY CIRCULATION

EXISTING SERVICE
AND STAFF CIRCULATION

FUTURE SERVICE
AND STAFF CIRCULATION

BALTIMORE MUSEUM OF ART, BALTIMORE, MARYLAND (2001) This site use and long-range space-planning study was undertaken to assist the Baltimore Museum of Art in determining the scope of future space relocations, renovations, and parking needs, as well as the potential future uses of all museum-owned off-site properties. Recommendations were made for the type and size of properties the museum might acquire in the future and how the museum facilities could better relate to Johns Hopkins University (JHU). > The 229,930-square-foot (21,360-square-meter) museum is located on a constrained site that is inflexibly defined by Art Museum Drive to the south, the JHU property line to the north, and the sculpture garden to the east. Very little space is available for building expansion. The west side of the site offers a small area to accommodate growth, but it is limited by an access road to JHU. > The project team was also challenged by the presence of the museum's historic centerpiece, a 1929 neoclassical building by architect John Russell Pope. The challenge was threefold. First, the Pope building presented an iconographic but non-functional entry at the center of the plan, located far from any actual entries. Second, the Pope building's classical symmetry implied, to some trustees, the concept that any expansion must directly follow its formal properties with a symmetrical format. The third challenge was the question of whether the museum campus should have an assemblage of styles representative of both the present and the multiple expansions of the past, or whether the campus should adopt an approach in which new additions are stylistically deferential to the neoclassical style of the Pope building. > The master plan's intention is to provide a balanced (although not necessarily symmetrical) growth to the east and west that optimizes interior circulation and maintains the visual centrality of the Pope building. Materials anticipated for use are limestone and clear glass on the additions adjacent to the Pope building, and red brick and glass, complementary to the Johns Hopkins material palette, on the north expansion. > The staff and board of the museum both requested that construction be divided into two phases due to funding and administrative priorities and limitations of financial resources. The initial phase contains a new lobby, expanded gift shop, renovated café, new temporary exhibition gallery, new library/study center, expanded art storage, and the enclosure of the Schaefer courtyard. A future phase provides additional and renovated space for galleries, administrative offices, registrarial areas, and exhibit preparation.

Existing main entry

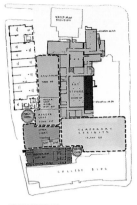

GROUND LEVEL PLAN

LEVEL TWO PLAN

LEVEL THREE PLAN

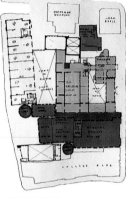

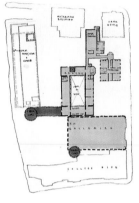

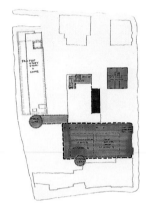

LEVEL FOUR PLAN

LEVEL FIVE PLAN

LEVEL SIX PLAN

Existing site view at future lobby

RHODE ISLAND SCHOOL OF DESIGN MUSEUM, PROVIDENCE, RHODE ISLAND (1999) The project team was asked by the RISD museum to analyze space needs and options in light of several problems, such as multiple "front" entries that all face a residential street; a serious lack of space for public areas, galleries, art handling, and education; a shortage of student resource or interactive areas; and an access-restricted, undersized loading area that faces the main public access path. > The resulting program and strategic plan provides a logical, functional, and economically feasible 15-year growth plan for the museum. The project increases the museum's size by 118,172 square feet (10,978 square meters), for a new museum total of 177,046 square feet (16,448 square meters). A new entry facing the rejuvenated riverwalk and the center city will help define the campus gateway. The expansion plans are the first step toward an integrated "central block" expansion plan that will also address the needs of the library, academic programs, and the relocation or expansion of the central power plant. > A critical component of the planning included the evaluation of potential reuse and related cost for both the Metcalf Building and Memorial Hall.

Existing museum

EXISTING GALLERY CIRCULATION

FUTURE GALLERY CIRCULATION

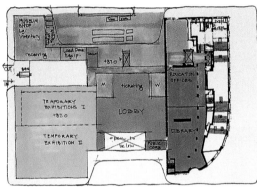

LEVEL TWO PLAN, FUTURE ENTRY OPTION

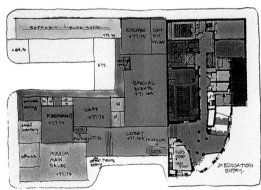

GROUND LEVEL PLAN, FUTURE ENTRY OPTION

SEATTLE ART MUSEUM, SEATTLE, WASHINGTON (1999) This project was initiated to evaluate the museum's long-range expansion needs, assisting the client in making real estate decisions regarding the use, disposition, and timing of development on the museum-owned adjacent properties. The study provided the client with a long-term financial analysis of assets, debt retirement, and future capital campaign needs regarding expansion costs, the operations endowment, and the acquisitions endowment. Various development alternatives were investigated, via site use and capacity studies based on zoning regulations and related floor area ratio requirements. > The programming, space-planning, and site master-planning components of the study were organized into both a ten-year and 20-year increment growth plan for the museum. The plan recommends expanding the Robert Venturi–designed building to the large site adjacent to the building on the north, while maintaining the parking structure across First Avenue as a revenue source and long-term land bank. The plan provides an increase of 197,500 square feet (18,348 square meters) for the ten-year need and 344,762 square feet (32,028 square meters) for the 20-year need, for a new museum total of 497,762 square feet (46,242 square meters). Major growth in new construction includes galleries, registrar areas, a dock, education space, a library, café, gift shop, and lobby. Major renovation recommendations focus primarily on education spaces and the area of the former gift shop. Other areas of the well-maintained Venturi design, particularly the galleries, will remain in place. > The museum will likely expand within the next ten to 15 years, although a building design was not included in this study.

85

TOP: Site model of future addition, sculpture garden, and on-site parking structure.
BOTTOM: Site model of future entry archway, gardens, and lobby.

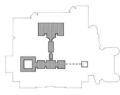

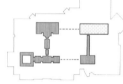

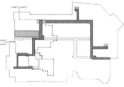

EXISTING GALLERY CIRCULATION   FUTURE GALLERY CIRCULATION   EXISTING SERVICE AND STAFF CIRCULATION   FUTURE SERVICE AND STAFF CIRCULATION

VIRGINIA MUSEUM OF FINE ARTS, RICHMOND, VIRGINIA (1998) Due to the consolidation of adjacent state properties, the Virginia Museum of Fine Arts (VMFA) site could be viewed as a single campus for the first time in its history. The master plan relocates surface parking lots from the heart of the site to a peripheral 600-car garage, and inserts sculpture gardens, fountains, an amphitheater, and landscaping to create an urban oasis. The site plan also unifies and integrates the site's neighboring buildings for the Virginia Historical Society, the VMFA Center for Education and Outreach, the historic Confederate Memorial Chapel, and the historic Robinson House. > The site plan is part of a comprehensive long-range plan to satisfy future museum needs over the next 20 to 30 years. > The existing facility, dating from 1935, never overcame its original split-level design, which resulted in roundabout and difficult circulation with numerous ramps and stairs between seven levels rather than four. The 132,000-square-foot (12,263-square-meter) expansion plan includes a new lobby, café, gift shop, and temporary exhibition galleries, as well as Asian and African permanent collection galleries. Service and art handling areas were also greatly expanded in the plan with new facilities for art storage, exhibition design, and production, objects conservation, painting conservation, and a photography studio. Many other departments were relocated into existing spaces for renovation, bringing the total facility plan to 569,500 square feet (52,907 square meters). >The expansion program resulted in major circulation improvements and a commitment to growth on the four most important levels, tripling the area of support space easily accessible to the dock. The plan also converted the gallery circulation pattern from a dead-end T-configuration to a complete loop, improving visitors' orientation and choices in gallery sequence. Changes to service area circulation greatly improved staff efficiency of art handling, art storage, registrar activities, and exhibit support activities. The art dock was separated from the non-art dock, reducing the use of ramped corridors by art handlers, while better distributing departments for less staff traffic in corridors. The building massing of the expansion diagram engages the urban garden, while creating welcoming, comfortable, and dramatic spaces within the building.

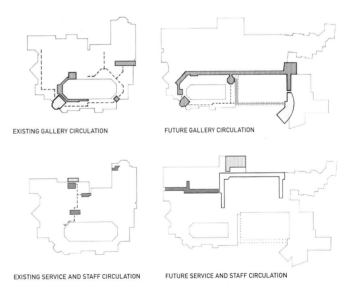

TOP: Original McNay house.
BOTTOM: Site model with future addition, parking structure, and sculpture garden.

MARION KOOGLER MCNAY ART MUSEUM, SAN ANTONIO, TEXAS (1997)

MARION KOOGLER MCNAY ART MUSEUM, SAN ANTONIO, TEXAS (1997) The Marion Koogler McNay Art Museum sought a site and museum master plan, space plan, and facilities evaluation to provide a logical, functional, and economically feasible growth plan through the year 2020. Since it opened in 1954, the museum has undergone eight separate expansion programs, each addressing individual departmental needs. This is the first comprehensive long-range plan to integrate all future needs. Therefore, major space-planning adjustments were required to provide a clear organization and plan for all departmental functions. > The original McNay house, dating from 1924, is built in a Spanish Colonial Revival style, and features portals, courtyards, and decorative tile-work. The space plan development responds to this architecture by organizing future growth around a second courtyard, and integrates portals and terraces to maximize views of the sculpture gardens, fountains, courtyards, and the beautifully landscaped 23-acre hilltop site. Through the use of limestone and plaster, the new design will serve as a contemporary complement to the original McNay house. > With the creation of separate and logical circulation paths for both public and service areas, the plan minimizes cross traffic and conflicting pathways for visitors, art handling, and food services. The project proposes an increase from 59,000 square feet to 132,903 square feet (12,347 square meters) by expanding primarily to the east, and includes a much needed new public entry. New construction includes a gallery for temporary exhibits, a special events area, a registrar's area, a dock, library, gift shop, and new entry. The total expansion plan was phased to match the institution's capital campaign recommendations, with the next major addition sized at 43,000 square feet (3,995 square meters). After new construction is completed, renovations of released space will follow. > A critical element of the master plan is already complete, with the construction of a central plant for chillers and boilers and the upgrading of gallery heating, venting, and air conditioning systems. New parking areas are also planned to increase capacity significantly.

EXISTING GALLERY CIRCULATION

FUTURE GALLERY CIRCULATION

EXISTING SERVICE AND STAFF CIRCULATION

FUTURE SERVICE AND STAFF CIRCULATION

87

CLOCKWISE FROM LEFT:
Site model of future additions. Model showing main entry. Model showing education entry. Model showing amphitheater, entry canopy, and main lobby. Elevation studies.

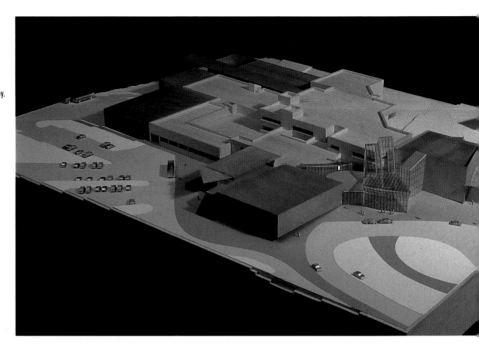

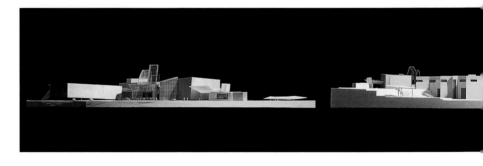

GROUND LEVEL DIAGRAM OF FUTURE USE

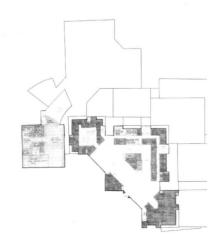

LEVEL TWO DIAGRAM OF FUTURE USE

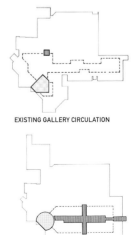

EXISTING GALLERY CIRCULATION

FUTURE GALLERY CIRCULATION

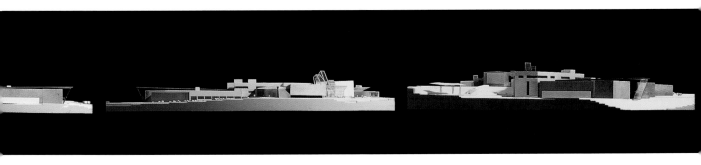

NORTH CAROLINA MUSEUM OF ART, RALEIGH, NORTH CAROLINA (1997) The North Carolina Museum of Art commissioned this study for an 82,000-square-foot (7,618-square-meter) expansion of Edward Durell Stone's original building. The expansion would allow the museum to grow to a total of 185,000 square feet (17,187 square meters), with a lively and revitalized public image that would serve the facility well into the 21st century. The programming, space-planning, and site master-planning project created a clear and logical circulation pattern for public and staff through a logical and economically feasible 20-year growth plan. > Major departmental expansion includes galleries, registrar areas, loading dock, educational facilities, a library, café, gift shop, and entry lobby. Major renovation will include administrative offices, curatorial facilities, external affairs, a special events area, galleries, the conservation department, and public program areas. The expansion and renovation recommendations also comprise code-compliance, new finishes, lighting upgrades, and the installation of a new fire-prevention system. > The existing façades are dominated by dark tinted glass and dark brown brick, appearing to many visitors as an impenetrable fortress for art. The master plan proposed that new materials have lighter colors and greater visibility into the museum to create a more welcoming image that clearly reveals the nature of interior public spaces for art, education, and community use. > The massing model conveys the potential use of metal, limestone, and clear glass, as well as the image of a museum in service to the people of North Carolina. This study, which helped the client obtain state funding, together with subsequent architectural studies and related financial evaluations, led to the acquisition of a new, adjacent site. The client is now pursuing a strategy that includes the development of a new, separate public wing for the lobby, auditorium, and gallery components. In this new scenario, the existing Edward Durell Stone building would remain as an administrative, service, and education wing.

89

URBAN PLANNING

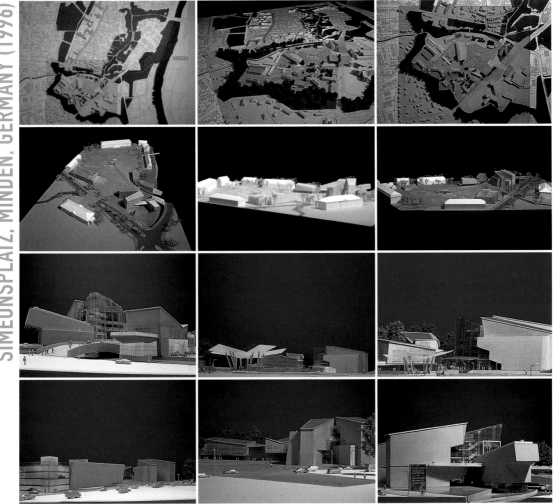

TOP ROW: Model of urban fabric. SECOND ROW: Model of plaza and perimeter buildings. THIRD ROW: Gateway between city center and Simeonsplatz with cinema and retail. BOTTOM ROW: Views of cinema and parking structure from Portastrasse.

SIMEONSPLATZ, MINDEN, GERMANY (1996) This project is the result of a commissioned competition, co-sponsored by a city planning department and an investor for the site's planned multiplex cinema. The RSA proposal was awarded first prize by vote of the professional and academic sectors of the jury, but was vetoed by the investor. The project "officially" received second place in the honorarium. This description indicates RSA's approach to the project. The Simeonskaserne Minden site is a void in the contemporary city fabric created by military occupancy since the Prussian era. Military use of the property created a secured boundary around which the city has grown. The goal in creating an urban design for this area is to engage the existing structure of the surrounding city and give it a presence on Simeonsplatz. Generating a new urban plaza (*platz*) that connects to the surrounding city fabric, the plan integrates existing circulation patterns and contributes new social spaces and urban activity. In addition to the design of the platz, the study develops the concept of "gateways," which programmatically and architecturally improve orientation, legibility, and use of the city. Thus, the design enhances, rather than obscures, the historic buildings and fortress, while creating an active urban center. > Four primary city infrastructures were identified as influences on the Simeonsplatz plaza and related buildings: (1) The City Center Gateway provides a portal to the main pedestrian path of the old city and its pedestrian-friendly assemblage of 17th- and 18th-century shop fronts. The plan calls for a new arching stone pathway to bridge over the existing creek, landing at a gateway formed by the entertainment and

91

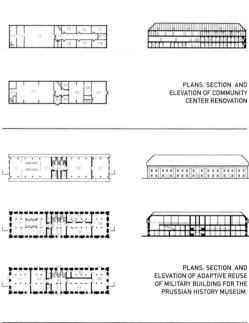

PLANS, SECTION, AND ELEVATION OF COMMUNITY CENTER RENOVATION

PLANS, SECTION, AND ELEVATION OF ADAPTIVE REUSE OF MILITARY BUILDING FOR THE PRUSSIAN HISTORY MUSEUM.

cinema buildings. (2) The Culture and Education Gateway consists of an elevated pedestrian bridge linked to a new amphitheater that is flanked by two historic buildings fronting Simeonsplatz. Adaptive reuse of these historic structures consist of a community center and a Prussian History Museum. The bridge spans the creek, providing a connection to the schools, kindergarten, and civic buildings along Königswall Street. (3) A mature greenbelt, formed by the 17th-century fortress walls, is one of the most recognizable and appreciated features of Minden. New landscaping and natural pathways that connect Simeonsplatz to the greenbelt are conceived as a Green Gateway. (4) A new urban lake surrounds the cinema buildings and gives the existing creek a symbolic presence on the site. Helping mask traffic noise from the heavily traveled Portastrasse, the water feature presents multilevel terraced waterfalls. > Simeonsplatz Center was created as the heart of the development concept, organizing the new buildings around a civic plaza and garden with views to each of the gateways and city infrastructure systems. The center includes a dramatic public pavilion exhibiting information about the city. > All new construction, including the parking structure, housing, shops, restaurants, and a multiplex cinema, integrate state-of-the-art energy technology, incorporating concepts of passive solar energy, waste heat recovery, and other renewable resource solutions. Five housing

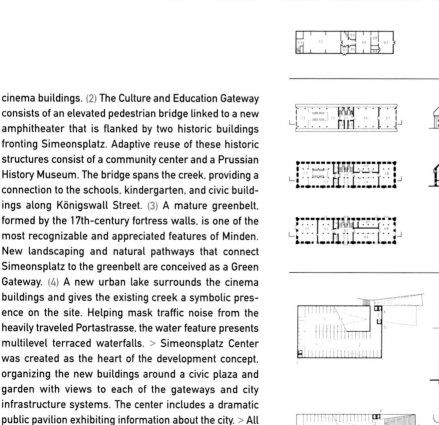

PLANS, SECTION, AND ELEVATION OF NEW PARKING STRUCTURE.

ELEVATION OF GATEWAY ORIENTED NORTH FROM PLAZA

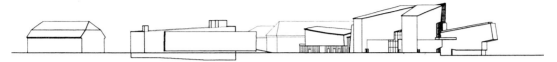

ELEVATION ORIENTED EAST FROM PORTASTRASSE

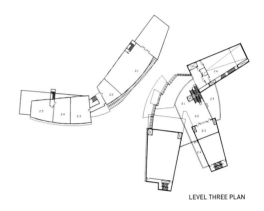

LEVEL THREE PLAN

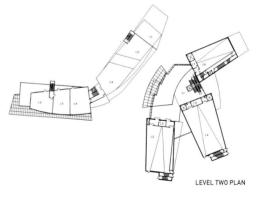

LEVEL TWO PLAN

blocks, varying in height from two to four levels, are clustered around five open courtyards. A variety of floor plan options are arranged in a total of 135 units that maximize natural light and views into the greenbelt. > The City Center Gateway design demonstrates in detail how site-specific building orientation can dramatically influence the connective aspect of urban design. The new cinema occupies the intersection of Portastrasse and Schwickowall, with theaters organized in three major blocks around a central atrium. The atrium is positioned to provide movie and restaurant patrons with views to and from the city and Simeonsplatz, while the theaters are situated to maximize the presence of the creek and urban lake. Separation of the theater blocks allows a building massing that integrates terraces, views, and natural light in every direction. The residual spaces between theater blocks create intimately scaled areas for food service, gift shop, ticketing, and lobby amenities. In response to the prominent urban site, the cinema building has articulated forms and views on all sides to create a 360-degree "front" without the blank rear façades that many cinemas have. The forms of the new plaster- and glass-clad buildings fan out toward Simeonsplatz, while standing seam metal roofs reach their maximum height at the gateway threshold. Plaza level façades have full-height glass for lobbies, entries, and retail display to animate and enliven the pedestrian experience.

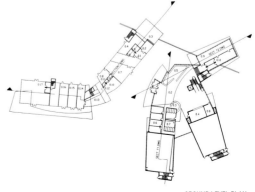

GROUND LEVEL PLAN

93

POST OAK CENTRAL—THESIS STUDY, HOUSTON, TEXAS (1989) RESEARCH FUNDED BY THE PITTMAN FELLOWSHIP AT RICE UNIVERSITY The study was undertaken at a time when Houston had approved localized light rail service in its most dense development zones including the study area of Galleria/Post Oak. Conventional planning proposals aligned the light rail with the prominent automobile street. This thesis provided a critical counterpoint to the city plan to use the light rail alignment as a device to force historical precedent (traditional pedestrian zones) onto this district. This design proposal sought a new urban form that more directly responded to the problem at hand. Houston's dispersed growth pattern exemplifies the post-suburban condition of mobility-driven development, the results of which led to areas of piecemeal mixed-use development along freeways and at major intersections. This has affected the grain of the city by deteriorating the once cohesive mixed-use activities of the downtown pedestrian environment and distributing the perimeter grain so broadly as to be accessible only by vehicular movement. The Galleria/Post Oak area was used as a case study for investigations in this urban form, providing insights into infrastructure and the correspondence between fast traffic roads, urban morphology, and the landscape. The urban morphology— or building and parking growth patterns—of this place strongly relates to the scale and speed of its road network, and negates the romantic notion of pedestrian promenades along shopping boulevards, an ideology which cannot be forced upon a place whose dominant traffic and parking pattern is too dispersed to support it. > The Galleria/Post Oak district took form during the late 1960s and early 70s. Initial developments were known as the Galleria, a mixed-use complex focused on an enclosed retail mall, and Smith Business Park, a linear grouping of office towers. The mall was located adjacent to a freeway exit at the crossing of two thoroughfares while the business park was located along the freeway access road. Due to their success, a number of other office parks, housing complexes, and strip retail/commercial buildings have developed along Post Oak Boulevard and the east-west thoroughfares it intersects. > Infrastructural hierarchy for movement is currently limited to the automobile and bus. There are three distinct levels of movement representing interaction at the scale of the city, district, and each autonomous development. These are represented by freeways, thoroughfares, and local access roads, respectively. Of these patterns the only one that approximates the scale of the traditional city is the local access roads, and many of these are privately owned with controlled access. > Building patterns can be distinguished by the separation of typologies. The commercial/retail pattern is primarily linear along Post Oak except at the regional mall. The towers follow two distinct patterns: linear for singular build-

ing projects primarily along Loop 610 and nodal for multiple building projects along Post Oak Boulevard. The nodal events are the only figural spaces in the area and each has a different use and character. > Acknowledging the nature of dispersing development patterns and their related automobile-dominated access is critical to the potential for a new form of public space and generative organizational patterns for future growth. This transformation of existing disparate typologies into an interconnected urban condition requires both the recognition of urban preconditions and an infrastructural intervention. > In the Galleria/Post Oak area the preeminent urban preconditions are found in the nodal development pattern and the three dominant typologies: (1) The first typology consists of the strip center and its dependence on large parking zones between the street and buildings; (2) The second typology consists of the retail mall and its internalized pedestrian street; and (3) The third typology consists of the high-rise building and adjacent garage with their symbolic front lawn and functional interface between them. > The distribution of these typologies follows a pattern similar to a branching diagram or flow chart. The use of these typologies in the Galleria/Post Oak area provides repetitive singular experiences that are the conscious choices of its users. This is unlike the pattern of the city grid, which allows plurality of use patterns and experiences. > Infrastructure of the proposed metro rail system and the locations of its four stops will solidify nodal patterning for the area. In the proposed plan these nodes result in both a horizontal and vertical conjuncture of typological conditions to create a dynamic urban condition. The proposed rail stops do not follow the existing pattern intrinsic to autonomous development that would cause each stop to itself become an isolated object. Instead the design locates the metro stops in conjunction with already established pedestrian patterns, both within the Galleria atrium and in transitional areas between parking structures and office towers. The rail stops themselves will generate additional pedestrian volume where it already exists and provides the momentum and economic basis for the emergence of adjacent spaces for shops, convenience amenities, and a new form of public space layered over private development.

OPPOSITE TOP: Aerial photo of the Post Oak site.
BOTTOM ROW, LEFT TO RIGHT: Diagram of Houston loop roads and development pockets. Perspective of metro stop exterior. Perspective of metro stop interior. Perspective from street level.

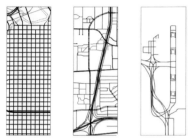   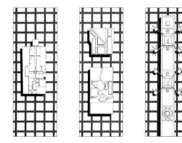

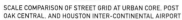 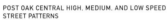

SCALE COMPARISON OF STREET GRID AT URBAN CORE, POST OAK CENTRAL, AND HOUSTON INTER-CONTINENTAL AIRPORT

POST OAK CENTRAL HIGH, MEDIUM, AND LOW SPEED STREET PATTERNS

SCALE COMPARISON OF POST OAK BUILDING TYPOLOGIES (GALLERIA AT LEFT, OFFICE PARK AT CENTER, AND AIRPORT TERMINAL AT RIGHT) OVERLAID WITH DOWNTOWN CITY GRID

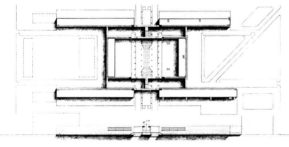 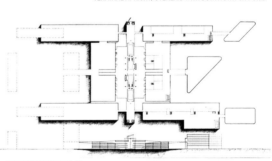

GROUND LEVEL PLAN

METRO STOP LEVEL PLAN

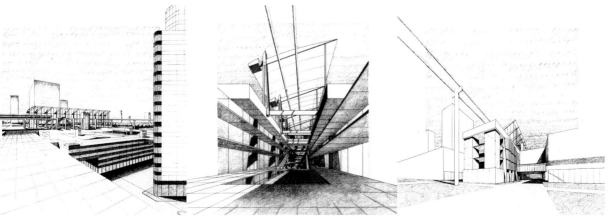

95

Computer simulation study of particle patterns by James Freeman of Fermi National Accelerator Laboratory (Fermilab) using the ISAJET model devised by Frank E. Paige, Jr. of Brookhaven National Laboratory.

SUPERCOLLIDER CITY, CENTRAL TEXAS (1988) The project to build the world's largest particle accelerator—and to provide a home for the associated new community of scientists and support industry required to operate the accelerator—was a leading candidate to be the nation's largest research effort since NASA. After garnering support from the Reagan Administration, the project was broadly debated in Congress but never received funding. The scientific aspect of the project design was complete by 1987. The urban and architectural planning was to have followed, with an anticipated date of operation in 1995. THE SCIENTIFIC EXPERIMENT: The Superconducting Supercollider (SSC) is an accelerator 20 times more powerful than any previous accelerator. It can probe matter in unprecedented detail, and re-create the conditions that prevailed near the beginning of time. The Supercollider tunnel, large enough to walk through and curved into a ring 52 miles around, lies buried below the earth's surface. Inside the tunnel is a small tramway for maintaining two cryogenic pipelines, each about two feet in diameter. Within each pipeline is a much smaller evacuated tube that carries a beam of protons, kept on course by the powerful superconducting magnets surrounding the tube. With

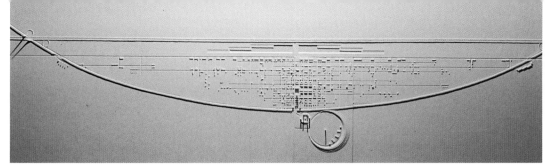

NEW TOWN MODEL

NEW TOWN CENTER SKETCH

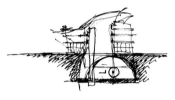

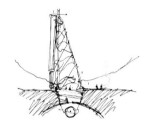

SECTION AND ELEVATION SKETCHES OF SCIENTIFIC BUILDINGS OVER TRACK ACCELERATOR

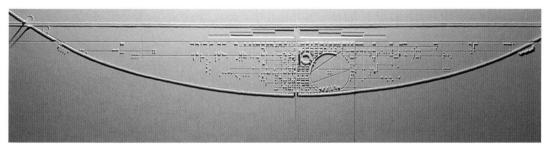

NEW TOWN MODEL—ALTERNATIVE CONFIGURATION

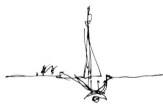

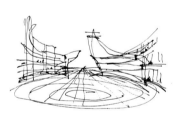

CENTER OBSERVATION TOWER AND PLAZA SKETCHES AT SCIENTIFIC CENTER

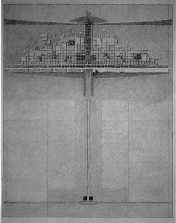

CITY PLANS

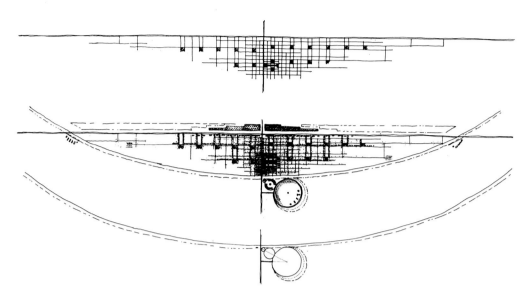

CONCEPTUAL DIAGRAM OVERLAYING SCIENTIFIC ELEMENTS AND COMMUNITY GRID

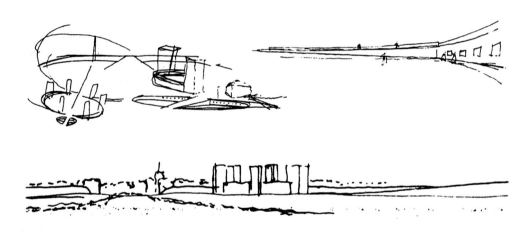

PERSPECTIVE SKETCHES

every circuit of the ring, the energy of the protons in the two-beam pipes is boosted by a pulse of radio waves; in 15 minutes the protons are accelerated around the ring in opposite directions more than three million times. Suddenly, electromagnetic gates are opened and the beam paths are made to cross. Pairs of protons collide, and some of the energy of the collision can be transferred at a rate that far exceeds the instantaneous output of all the power plants on the earth into a region whose diameter is 100,000 times smaller than the diameter of a proton. New elementary particles that could materialize from the energy may show how to explain the origin of subatomic mass.

THE PROGRAM: The project called for designers to investigate strategies for the inception and development of a new "town," with an initial population of 4,000 residents and eventual growth to 20,000 or more. Scientific components of the town plan included a central office and laboratory complex, support and maintenance buildings, a fire and security building, and warehouses. A broad spectrum of civic facilities were included, encompassing a 10,560-square-foot (981-square-meter) town hall, a 13,992-square-foot (1,300-square-meter) library, a police station, an elementary

98

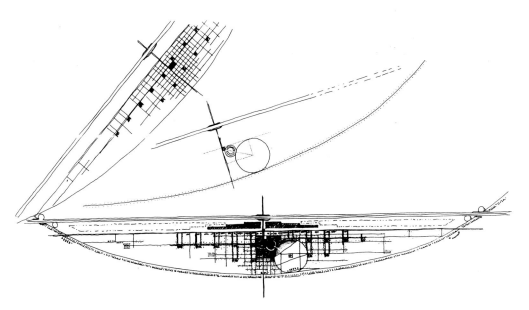

CONCEPTUAL DIAGRAM OVERLAYING SCIENTIFIC ELEMENTS AND COMMUNITY GRID—ALTERNATIVE CONFIGURATION

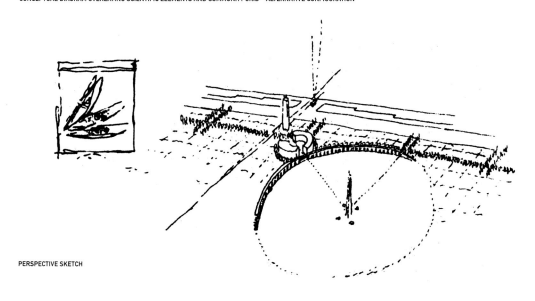

PERSPECTIVE SKETCH

school, a 7,790-square-foot (724-square-meter) recreation and community center, a post office, a fire station, and parks. A range of institutional facilities included churches, research facilities, and a future hospital. Commercial facilities comprised retail components, a cinema, fast food restaurants, service stations, office warehouse facilities, a future hotel, and parking. Staffing for all of these venues was housed in a wide variety of residential facilities, made up of 30 percent apartments, 70 percent single family houses (at all price levels), and a mobile home park.   As Texas was the leading candidate state for the SSC, the project master plan was created on a featureless plain 30 miles west of a major metropolis, near a freeway and an older highway. The parti was to make evident the scientific components (the booster tracks and collider ring) within the traditional city morphology. This was done in order to create a dialogue between tradition and technology that would be informed by the town's very reason for existence. Two designs were pursued: one organized the scientific components tangentially within the urban fabric, and the other, preferred scheme layered the geometry of the scientific components with the urban fabric.

IN PROGRESS

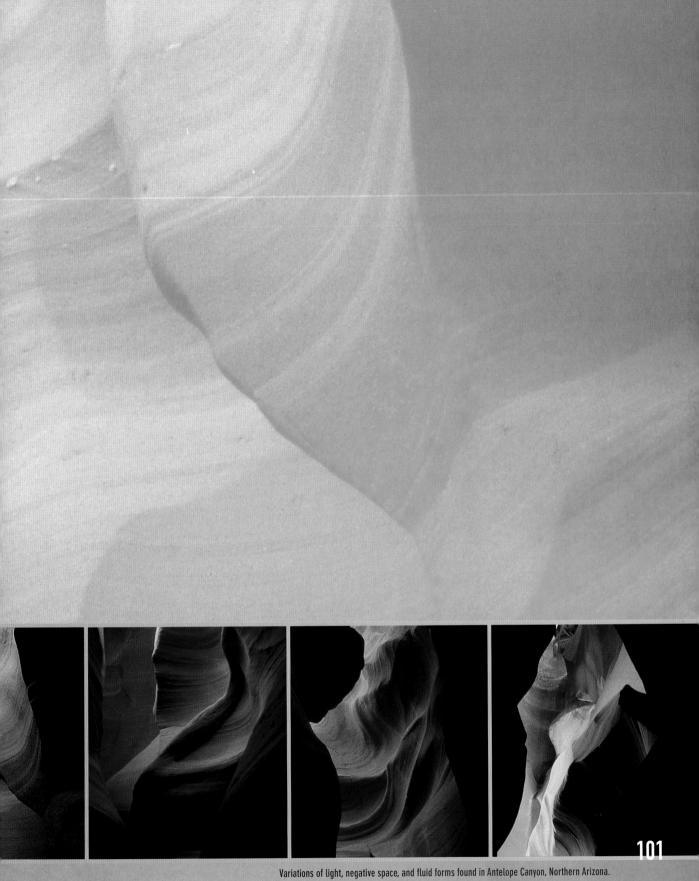

Variations of light, negative space, and fluid forms found in Antelope Canyon, Northern Arizona.

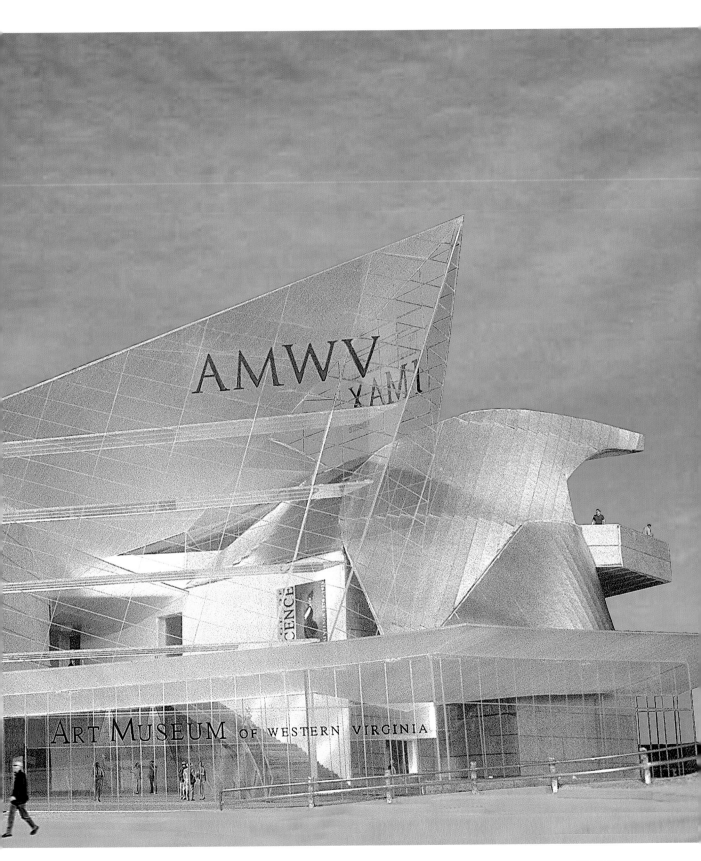

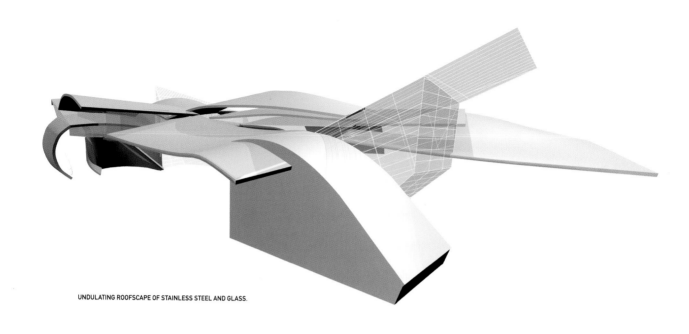

UNDULATING ROOFSCAPE OF STAINLESS STEEL AND GLASS.

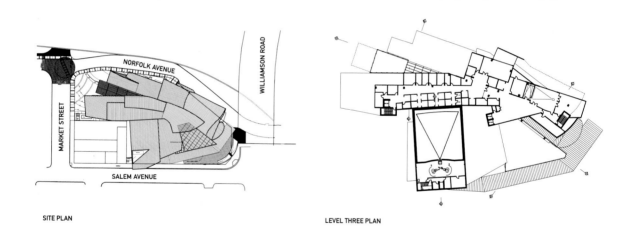

SITE PLAN

LEVEL THREE PLAN

PREVIOUS PAGES: Main entry at the gateway to downtown Roanoke. BELOW, LEFT TO RIGHT: View of the lobby and boardroom terrace from Williamson Road. Entry canopy and lobby atrium. Northeast elevation from Williamson Road.

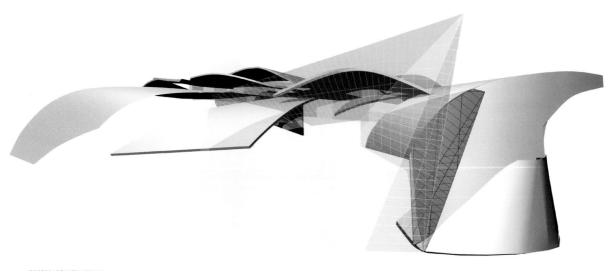

ROOFSCAPE WITH ATRIUM

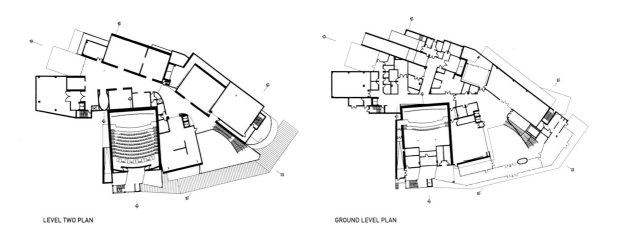

LEVEL TWO PLAN

GROUND LEVEL PLAN

ART MUSEUM OF WESTERN VIRGINIA AND THE ADVANCE AUTO PARTS IMAX THEATRE, ROANOKE, VIRGINIA (2006) Located on the prominent north-west corner of Roanoke's downtown, the new Art Museum of Western Virginia and IMAX facilities create a physical and iconographic gateway into the city for visitors arriving from U.S. Highway 581. As the city's most contemporary structure, it also represents Roanoke's metaphorical gateway to the future, as the city transforms its financial basis from an industrial and manufacturing economy to a technology information and services driven one. The building's forms and materials interpret the renowned beauty and drama of the surrounding landscape of the Shenandoah Valley framed by the Blue Ridge and Appalachian Mountains. > The building will house collections focused on 18th- and 19th-century American art, contemporary art, Southern decorative art, prints and photographs, and non-western art. The facility will contain advanced technology for distance learning to serve the entire region of western Virginia through a cooperative program with nearby Virginia Tech. It will also feature fiber-optic cable links with Network

105

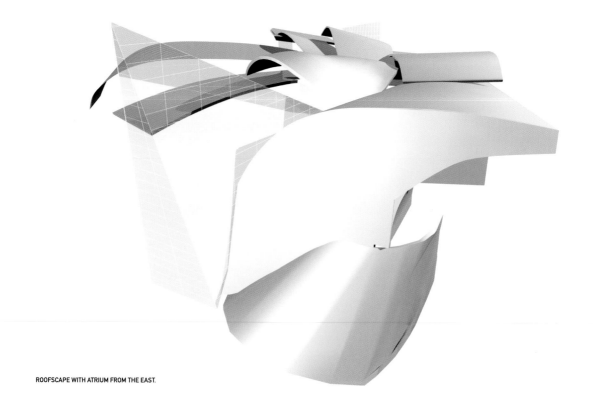

ROOFSCAPE WITH ATRIUM FROM THE EAST.

ABOVE LEFT: View from Williamson Road southbound. ABOVE RIGHT: View from U.S. 581 looking west.

Virginia in order to enhance secondary education access to the arts. The museum will also link with Virginia Tech to provide artistic endeavors via the university's computer automated virtual environment (CAVE). > The 70,000-square-foot (6,503-square-meter) building occupies three levels. The facility's primary public spaces, including the museum lobby, IMAX lobby, café, gift shop, auditorium, and education spaces, are located on the ground level, as are the support areas associated with the loading dock and art-receiving activities. The permanent collection galleries, temporary exhibit galleries, and art storage are located on the second level. The third and uppermost floor holds the boardroom, director's suite, and all staff offices. Representing the hub for the entire facility, the museum atrium rises to a height of 75 feet (23 meters). > The building will contain sustainable design components such as daylighting, passive solar, thermal conserving envelope, and computerized building management systems. The project is scheduled to start construction in spring 2005.

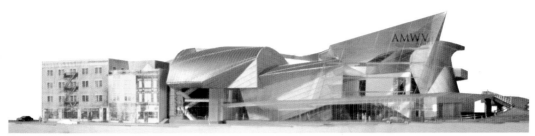

SOUTH ELEVATION FROM SALEM AVENUE

NORTH ELEVATION FROM NORFOLK AVENUE

WEST ELEVATION FROM MARKET STREET

EAST ELEVATION FROM US581

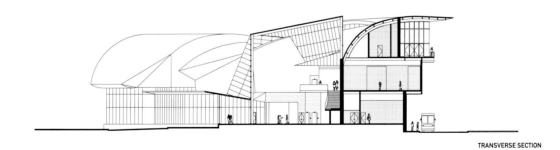

TRANSVERSE SECTION

LONGITUDINAL SECTION

ART MUSEUM OF WESTERN VIRGINIA < IN PROGRESS

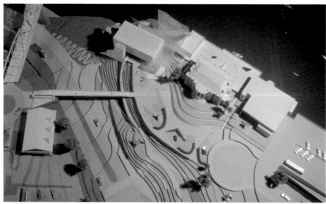

ABOVE, FROM TOP: Aerial view of site model. View from future pedestrian bridge. View across Tennessee River. OPPOSITE: Flowing roof forms lead the visitor through the entry into the main lobby. BELOW LEFT: Existing 1905 mansion and 1973 museum addition. BELOW RIGHT: Bluff edge of new west addition.

HUNTER MUSEUM OF AMERICAN ART, CHATTANOOGA, TENNESSEE (2005) Dramatically situated atop an 80-foot limestone bluff overlooking the Tennessee River and downtown Chattanooga, the new Hunter Museum of American Art will be one of the most prominent buildings in the city. The new building rises over 45 feet above the bluff, with an easily recognizable profile and clear sight lines from the city's historic core and from across the river into the building's public features, such as lobby, view terraces, and sculpture gardens. > The architects developed the building form's design imagery from the rock outcroppings and strata of the cliffs underneath. The river's dynamic movement finds its metaphor in the lobby roof glazing separating the mass of the new construction from the existing buildings. > Conceived as primarily a west addition to the historic 1905 mansion, expanded to the north and east in the 1970s, the project brings balance to the overall facility and site composition and reestablishes the primacy of the mansion at the center of the complex. The new building seeks to reach out to the larger community by its intriguing, welcoming forms, extensive public areas, sociable terraces, and numerous city-watching plazas and balconies. > The program for civic engagement is further extended via a new pedestrian bridge. The bridge connects a new public plaza at Walnut Street and First Street to the museum, allowing visitors to walk above the traffic from the city to the museum. This revitalized

109

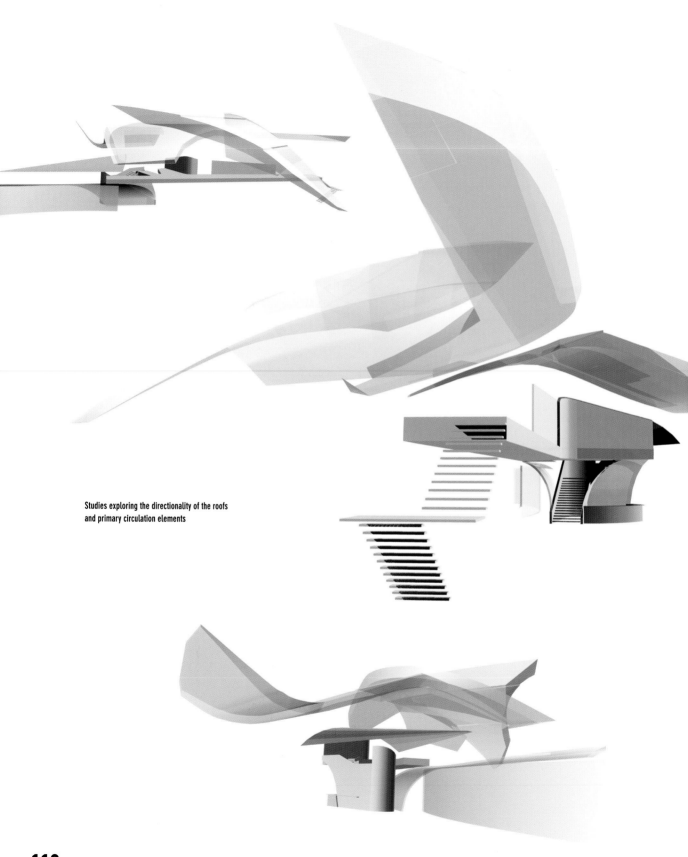

Studies exploring the directionality of the roofs
and primary circulation elements

110

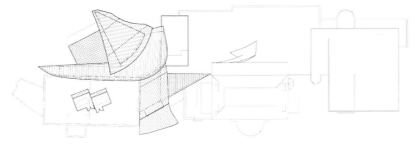

ROOF PLAN

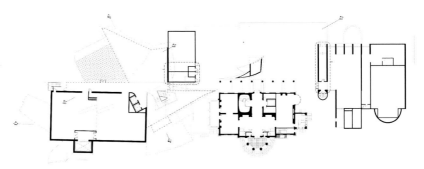

LEVEL TWO PLAN

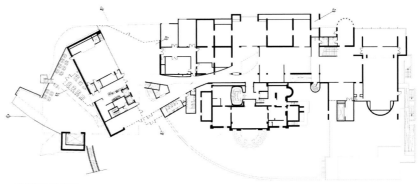

GROUND LEVEL PLAN

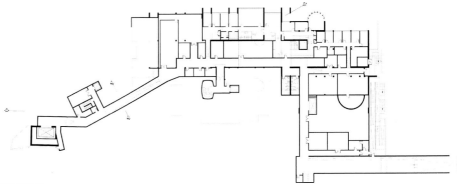

LOWER LEVEL PLAN

111

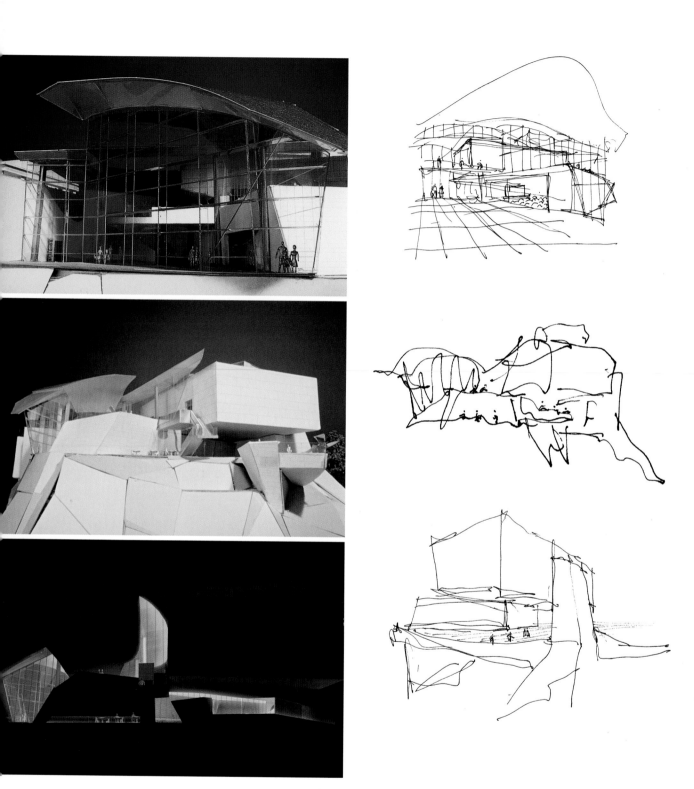

FROM TOP: View into lobby atrium at the north edge of the bluff. Outreaching forms create multiple opportunities for sculpture terraces and view decks over the bluff's edge. At night, the building glows from within. OPPOSITE TOP: South elevation view of the sculpture garden plaza, new west addition, and historic mansion.

112

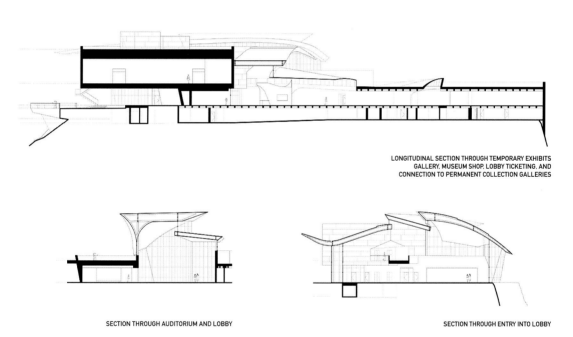

LONGITUDINAL SECTION THROUGH TEMPORARY EXHIBITS
GALLERY, MUSEUM SHOP, LOBBY TICKETING, AND
CONNECTION TO PERMANENT COLLECTION GALLERIES

SECTION THROUGH AUDITORIUM AND LOBBY

SECTION THROUGH ENTRY INTO LOBBY

urban prospect reverses the site's previous isolation, created when Riverfront Drive was excavated in the 1970s. The contemporary language of the 2005 addition will be a dramatic contrast to the museum's original 1905 mansion home. It transfers the museum's public image from that of a private, reserved manor to a lively, open civic forum for all the arts. The new building will also act as a notable tourist attraction for the city's newly revitalized downtown and riverfront. > The plan removes the surrounding surface parking to create a museum encompassed by gardens, outdoor sculpture, and public access view terraces. New public areas, including the lobby, auditorium, education studios, café, and gift shop, are consolidated on the main gallery level to improve the visitor experience. This dedicates the lower level to administrative and museum support areas. A new temporary exhibitions gallery will be located above the auditorium, with views into the lobby atrium and toward the river. A new below-grade loading dock minimizes delivery traffic presence on the site and supports a new suite of spaces for registrarial receiving, exhibit preparation, security, and art storage. > The anticipated materials palette includes opaque building areas clad in native stone, providing the impression of the building emerging from the stone bluff. The lobby and adjacent glazed wall areas will have clear insulated glass in aluminum frames and a translucent polycarbonate roof over galvanized structural steel.

113

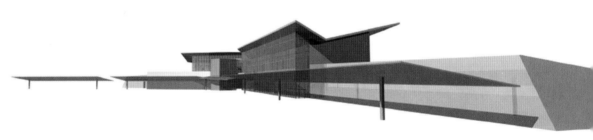

POLICE STAFF ENTRY.

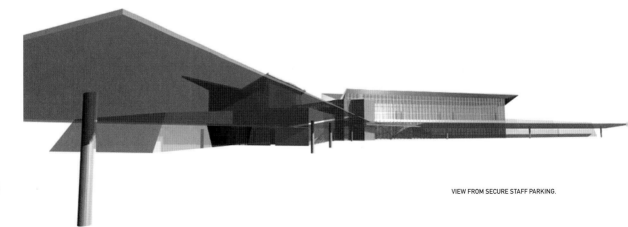

VIEW FROM SECURE STAFF PARKING.

ABOVE: South elevation from Arrow Highway. BELOW: Aerial views of the site model.

MONTCLAIR POLICE STATION, MONTCLAIR, CALIFORNIA (2005) With the jagged peaks of the San Gabriel Mountains and imposing Mount Baldy framing the backdrop to the north, the crested and folded roof plates of the Montclair Police Station look over the city to the south. The site design provides public garden space on the prominent southwest corner, where Arrow Highway intersects Central Avenue. The public use of the site, together with the clear glass lobby and engaging building forms, combine to provide a welcoming and receptive facility to complement the Montclair Police Department's community-based policing program. > The 38,000-square-foot (3,530-square-meter) plan contains state-of-the-art policing facilities and technology with dispatch and briefing rooms, an Emergency Operations

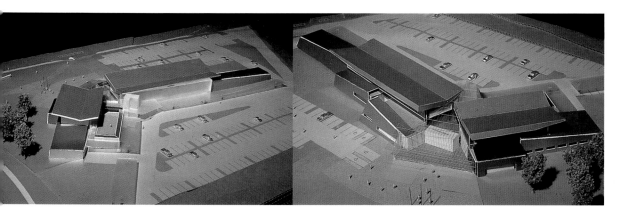

115

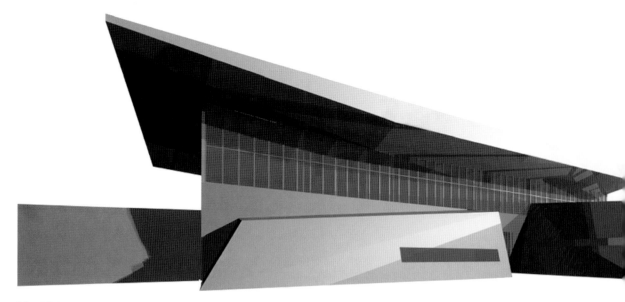

Police staff wing.

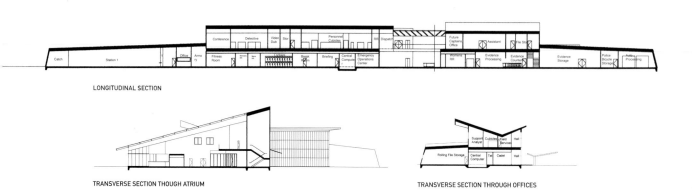

LONGITUDINAL SECTION

TRANSVERSE SECTION THOUGH ATRIUM

TRANSVERSE SECTION THROUGH OFFICES

Center, detainee and evidence processing, a detective bureau, administrative offices, records storage, a shooting range, conference rooms, and fitness areas. Within the building, secure zones are organized with staff circulation on a north corridor to take advantage of mountain views, visibility of the secure patrol parking area, and shade from the desert-like inland sun. On the south façades, dramatic overhangs are sized to admit the low winter sun and provide shade during the remainder of the year. > The exterior materials relate to the low-cost, high durability, and high-tech aesthetic often associated with policing equipment. The building cladding of clear aluminum corrugated siding, metallic blue metal siding, and clear glass with aluminum frames creates a refreshing contrast to the stucco and tilt-up precast concrete that are prevalent in other moderate cost buildings in the area.

BELOW: Model photos. OPPOSITE BELOW: Staff entrance.

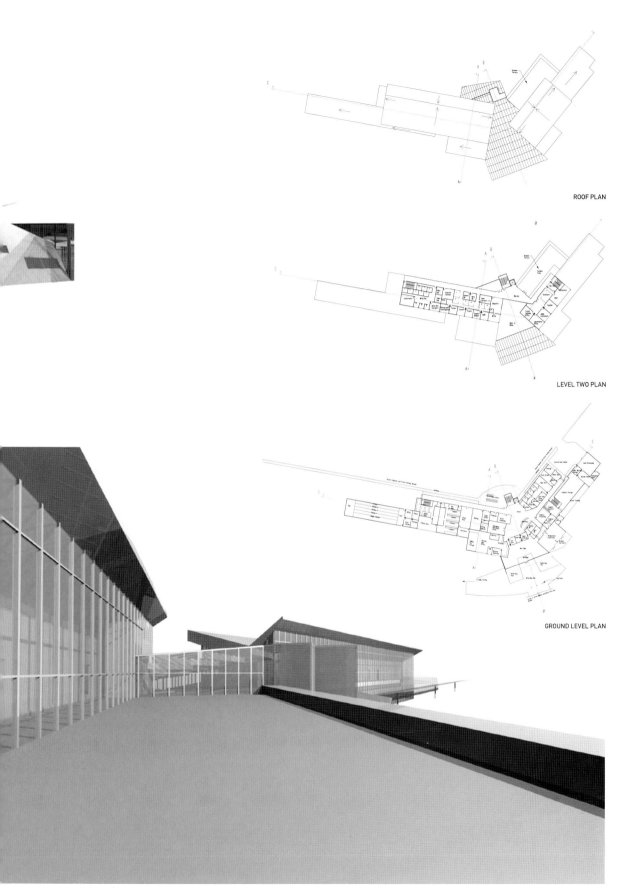

ROOF PLAN

LEVEL TWO PLAN

GROUND LEVEL PLAN

117

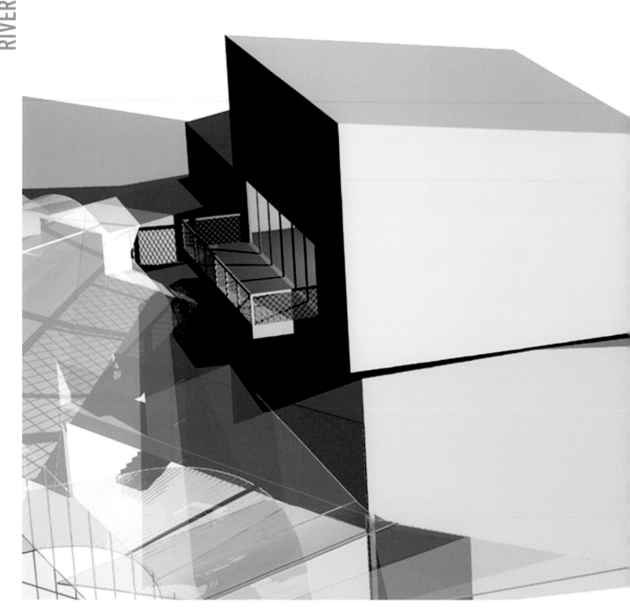

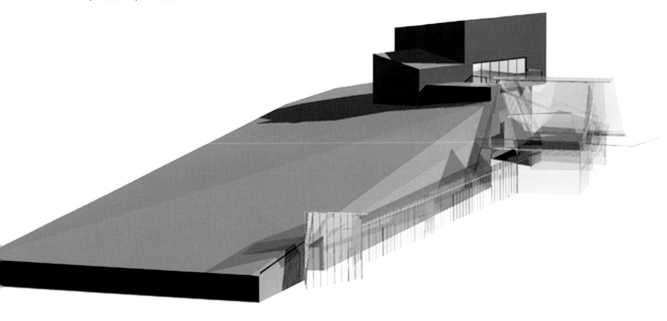

UNIVERSITY OF CALIFORNIA, RIVERSIDE, ALUMNI AND VISITORS CENTER,
RIVERSIDE, CALIFORNIA (2005) The new University of California,
Riverside, Alumni and Visitors Center is a 38,297-
square-foot (3,558-square-meter) building slated to
begin construction in the winter of 2004. Prominently
located at the campus' ceremonial entrance, the center
forms a new gateway to the arts-oriented north campus.
Sited on an east-west axis, the new Alumni Center will,
along with the Fine Arts Building, create a "gateway"
into the Fine Arts Mall. At the same time the buildings
encourage campus growth to the west, while establishing the edge to a new pedestrian zone that will eventually face the Performing Arts Center. > The Alumni and
Visitors Center will serve as a campus facility providing
space for the diverse needs of alumni, visitors, faculty,
students, staff, and other university support groups.
The facility will provide a banquet hall, lobby, alumni
library, meeting rooms, executive boardroom, full service kitchen, café, auditorium, administrative offices, the
University Club, and the Student Services Department
tour center. > While primarily a one-story building, the
facility's roof rises from east to west, with enough volume at its apex to accommodate administrative offices
on a partial second level. Appearing to hover above the
main roof, a third level boardroom and deck allow views

119

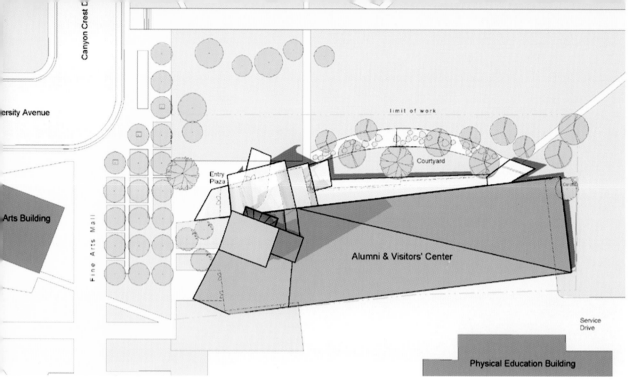

SITE PLAN

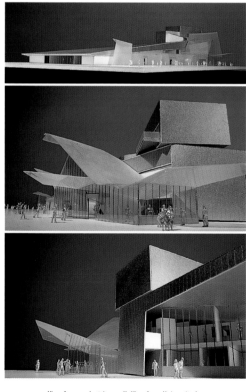

TOP TO BOTTOM: View from pedestrian mall. View from University Avenue.
View from Fine Arts Pedestrian Mall.

of the surrounding mountains. Additional features of the massing include a high-volume lobby and dramatic overhangs, which shelter the entries for the main lobby, the University Club, and tour group queuing, as well as the courtyard. > Two major material and formal compositions comprise the building's design. The first is a background formation whose walls and roof are clad in warm gray cement panels that relate in color to the stone of the surrounding mountains as well as the tan brick and stucco used predominantly throughout campus. This formation is volumetrically faceted and inclined in response to the surrounding mountains and rock outcroppings. In the foreground of the composition, a series of sweeping and curvilinear planes of translucent polycarbonate sheeting and clear glass contain the prominent public circulation spaces. > The building has a very simple linear plan with two key features. In the first, the primary public spaces (lobby, living room, café, and public corridor) are located at the most visible and accessible corner of the site. This area of the site connects to the terminus of University Avenue and is directly south of the access to a major visitor parking structure. The second feature is a food service plan that serves as a "hub," with convenient and efficient access to the many dining/multipurpose venues in the building.

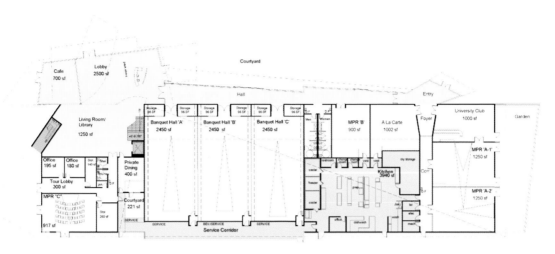

GROUND LEVEL PLAN

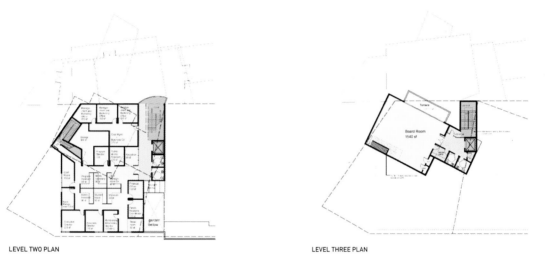

LEVEL TWO PLAN

LEVEL THREE PLAN

LONGITUDINAL SECTION

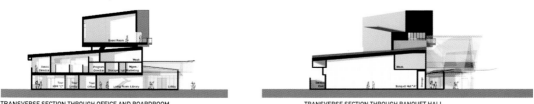

TRANSVERSE SECTION THROUGH OFFICE AND BOARDROOM

TRANSVERSE SECTION THROUGH BANQUET HALL

121

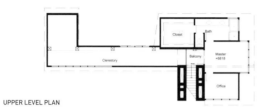

UPPER LEVEL PLAN

ABOVE: **Existing site after it was ravaged by fire.**

BELOW. CLOCKWISE FROM TOP LEFT: **View from terrace. View from entry drive. South Elevation. North Elevation.**

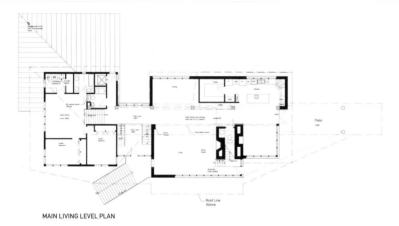

MAIN LIVING LEVEL PLAN

LOWER LEVEL PLAN

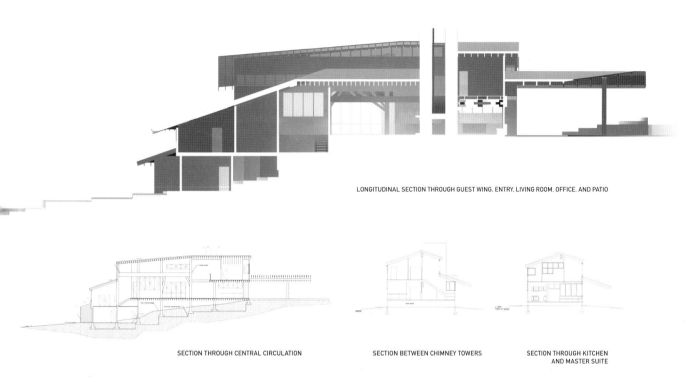

LONGITUDINAL SECTION THROUGH GUEST WING, ENTRY, LIVING ROOM, OFFICE, AND PATIO

SECTION THROUGH CENTRAL CIRCULATION

SECTION BETWEEN CHIMNEY TOWERS

SECTION THROUGH KITCHEN AND MASTER SUITE

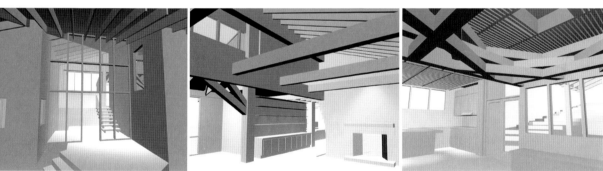

LEFT TO RIGHT: Entry. Living Area. Dining and Kitchen.

BLAIR RESIDENCE, DURANGO, COLORADO (2004) This project design was initiated in the ashes of a devastating wildfire that scorched the heavily wooded, 50-acre mountain site overlooking the Animas Valley, six miles north of Durango. The client lost two homes in the fire but choose to rebuild with rugged determination. As hundreds of burned Ponderosa pines were removed from the site, newly opened panoramic views were revealed in the barren topography. Hugging the ridgeline, the building forms yield dramatic southerly valley and northerly mountain views. > The fire's widespread destruction drastically changed the region's physical environment and the site's ancient trees are only a memory. To assuage their longing for the original landscape, the client agreed with the architect on a building palette that returns aged and indigenous colors and materials to the site. The exterior roof is clad in rusted Cor-Ten steel, and exterior walls are of local stone (similar to nearby Mesa Verde) and weathered wood planks. The building forms respond in a way that allows the stone to serve as a ruin-like base to support the contemporary construction above. > Four levels allow the 5,300-square-foot (492-square-meter) house to transition up the ridge, with the garage at the lowest level, a guest bedroom wing at the second level, the main living level above that, and the top floor serving as the retreat for the master bedroom and office. The plan's organization allows not only maximum views but also excellent orientation for natural cross-ventilation from prevailing southerly breezes and south over-hangs for sunlight control. > The interiors feature heavy timber framing, stone fireplaces, and corner window detailing. The use of native materials gives the home a sense of being rooted to its place, while the clean and contemporary application of form and detail make it clearly a building of its time.

123

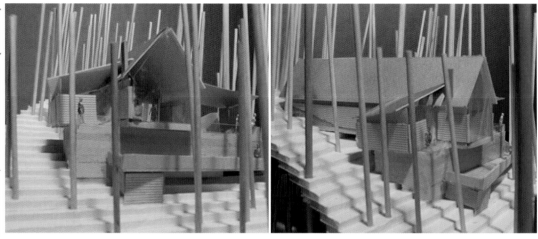

ABOVE LEFT: Concept model north elevation. ABOVE RIGHT: Concept model east elevation.

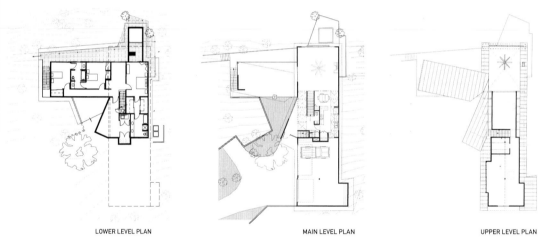

LOWER LEVEL PLAN

MAIN LEVEL PLAN

UPPER LEVEL PLAN

SITE VEGETATION

WASSON RESIDENCE, NORRIS, TENNESSEE (2004) Sited on a densely wooded north slope that faces the land preserve surrounding Norris Lake, this residence provides a contemporary interpretation of the beautifully crafted wooden barns in the region. Most meaningful among these barns is the circa 1903 Mynatt Barn, built by Marcia Wasson's great-grandfather and subsequently expanded by her grandfather in the early 1950s. Referencing barn cantilevers, continuous eave vents, and steeply gabled roofs, this house appears to have evolved from indigenous agricultural forms that maximize natural ventilation while being distinctly contemporary in its overall composition. > Organized so that it is elevated above the sloping terrain, the living room sits just below the leafy canopy of oak, maple, and poplar trees. The room is reminiscent of a tree house, with permanently protected views toward the forest. Bedrooms and a fitness area are located on a

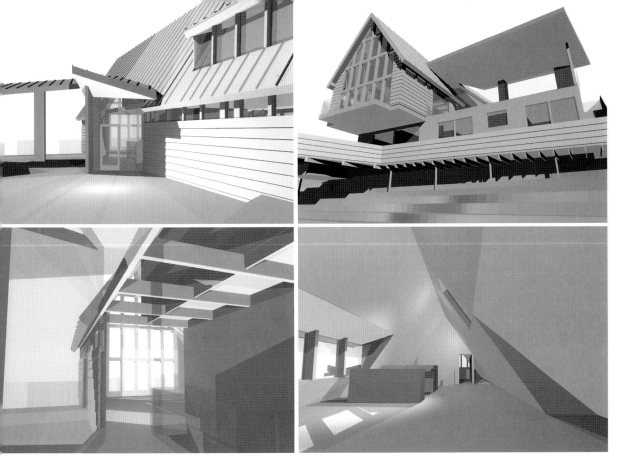

CLOCKWISE FROM TOP LEFT: Entry. View of north façade. View toward living area from entry. Loft interior.

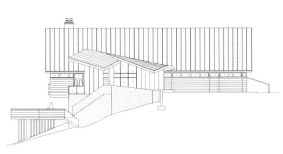

WEST ELEVATION

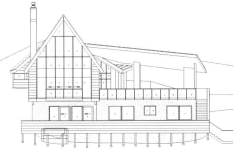

NORTH ELEVATION

lower level with a private terrace and jacuzzi that also face the forest. An upper level loft provides a playroom and a study/retreat that overlooks the living room. > Clad primarily in cedar, the walls of the house blend in color with the neutral tones of the forest, while galvanized metal roof forms catch the sunlight filtering through the treetops. The interior spaces are rendered predominantly in wood, glass, and white gypsum board. Sliding glass doors in the tall glass wall of the living room open to the north to bring indoors the views of surrounding woodlands and glimpses of the nearby wildlife. At the same time the opening glass walls deliver cool mountain breezes inside. Sliding glass doors also open to the west toward a covered entertainment terrace. > The residence contains 5,012 square feet (465 square meters) of enclosed space plus 1,300 square feet (121 square meters) of terraces and decks.

SITE PLAN

125

UNBUILT

127

Layered geometric patterns of form and light found in lobster traps, Portland, Maine.

EXISTING SITE

CONCEPT SKETCH

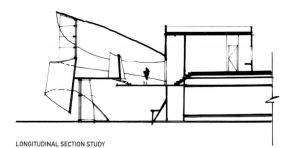

TRANSVERSE SECTION STUDY

LONGITUDINAL SECTION STUDY

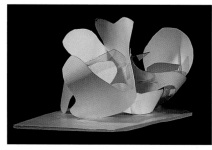
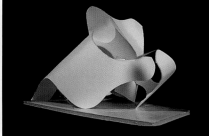
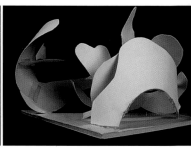

MATLIN RESIDENCE, VENICE, CALIFORNIA (2000) Located on a tight site in Venice, the new owner of this existing triplex sought to create a personal residence that conveyed the qualities of her own fine arts photography. With an extraordinarily creative eye for composition and freedom from conventional attitudes toward residential form, the client participated in a design process that led to a single, free-flowing three-dimensional form that defines the primary exterior and interior walls. Fitted within this flowing form were the living room, kitchen, dining room, and a studio space. The existing apartments were to be gutted and refitted as a guest apartment and the master bedroom. > The curving wall, clad in flat seamed aluminum panels, contrasts with the more utilitarian sealed concrete floors and plywood cabinetry of the interior. Large glass walls yield garden views from the lower level and distant mountain views from the upper levels. The renovated portions of the existing triplex are clad in corrugated aluminum sheeting, providing a contrast of texture and reflection with the smooth aluminum surface of the curved walls. New construction areas total 1,600 square feet (149 square meters), and renovated areas contain 980 square feet (91 square meters).

128

ABOVE: Façade of primary living spaces. BELOW: Views of conceptual model, paper. BOTTOM LEFT AND RIGHT: Elevation view of model.

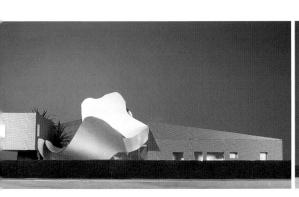
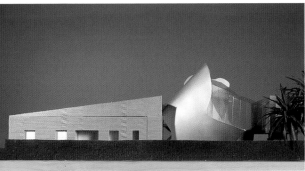

129

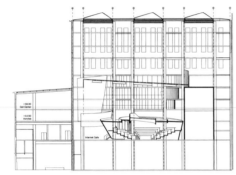

LONGITUDINAL SECTION

TELEOS TELECOM HEADQUARTERS, KIRCHLENGERN, GERMANY (1998) The adaptive reuse of an abandoned 1915 power plant provides a dramatic setting for the corporate headquarters of Teleos, a telecommunications company. > The new design evolves out of a dialogue between the structure's history and future. Originally erected to contain gigantic machinery, such as boilers, burners, pumps, and pipes, the impressive steel skeleton of huge, bolted I-beams and 130-foot-high (40-meter-high) columns presents memories of the early industrial technology of the past century. The structure's future use is as an office building for a company whose technology points into the new millennium. The project contrasts the physical energy of heavy industry that once circulated through the building with the more virtual energy of telecommunication.> The building's new forms play against the massive shapes of the building's former function. Compositions of cylindrically curved metal elements, reminiscent of the building's original boilers and smokestacks, juxtapose to communicate across the open atrium. The designers used various configurations of these partial cylinders to create the new exterior entry and conference facilities. The combination of materials—stainless steel,

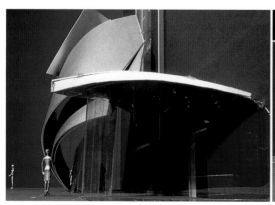

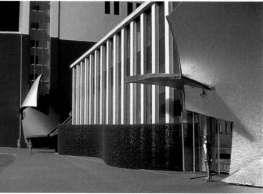

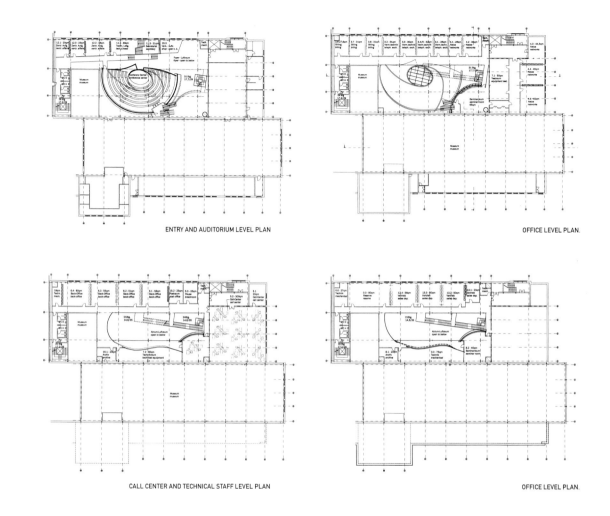

ENTRY AND AUDITORIUM LEVEL PLAN

OFFICE LEVEL PLAN.

CALL CENTER AND TECHNICAL STAFF LEVEL PLAN

OFFICE LEVEL PLAN.

OPPOSITE ABOVE LEFT: Existing building and context. OPPOSITE ABOVE RIGHT: Interior view of decommissioned power plant. OPPOSITE BELOW LEFT: New entry canopy and vestibule. OPPOSITE BELOW RIGHT: Exterior view. BELOW LEFT: Atrium and main stair. BELOW RIGHT: Auditorium interior.

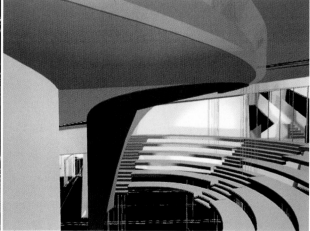

131

ABOVE, CLOCKWISE FROM TOP LEFT: Lower level of atrium. Internet café. Atrium and auditorium. Internet café with reception beyond. BELOW: Lighting studies in conference rooms. OPPOSITE ABOVE TOP: Structural studies of entry canopy. BOTTOM ROW: Auditorium model.

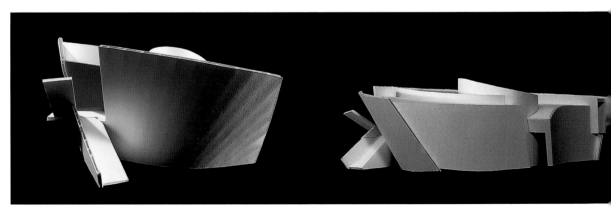

transparent glass, polycarbonate panels, and the hovering, cantilevered forms—creates an ethereal feel within the massive shell. > The historic brick façades are cleaned and renovated with new aluminum-framed windows and enhanced with a sculptural entry foyer. Inside the building, the central atrium contains a 115-seat auditorium, conference room, and seminar room. Residual spaces between these atrium objects further serve as a lobby reception area, internet café, and sales shop, which are all open for public use. > Perimeter offices are located along the heavily windowed west façade. The 3,230-square-foot (300-square-meter) call-switching center is located on the north side, with 16.4-foot-high (five-meter-high) ceilings and ample windows. The walls and floors, through the use of murals and custom-designed carpet, are wrapped with a super-graphic image of the company's "Solar Constellation" logo. Rooms for archives, mechanical systems, and technical equipment are located along the east side of the building, which is windowless below the 92-foot (28-meter) level. The aggregate project area contains 100,000 square feet (9,290 square meters) of newly renovated space.

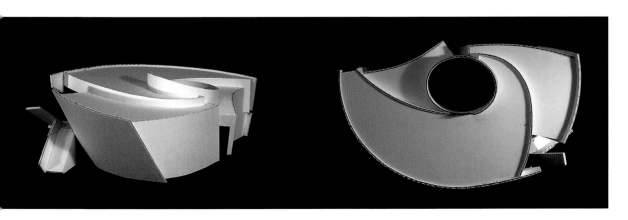

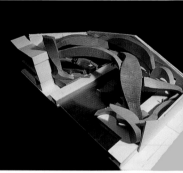

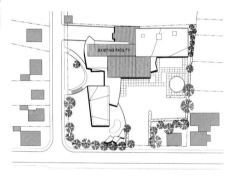

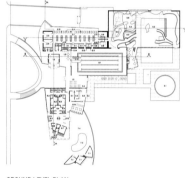

LEFT, TOP ROW: Existing facility.
BELOW: Context model with proposed addition (left and center). Arial view of fantasy pool forms (right).
OPPOSITE : Fantasy pool interior.

ENGER NATATORIUM, ENGER, GERMANY (1997)

SITE PLAN

GROUND LEVEL PLAN

ENGER NATATORIUM, ENGER, GERMANY (1997) This project for the expansion and renovation of the existing Enger Natatorium is located on the town's Ringstrasse at the western edge of a large recreational park. The client requested that the facility be enlarged to a total of 39,623 square feet (3,681 square meters) and upgraded to compete with new natatoriums recently built in neighboring communities. The program included a sauna, fitness facility, and family-oriented fantasy pool with active water features. In Germany, these fantasy pools are often literal representations of resort destinations. In this case, the fantasy pool consists of abstracted arches and curving forms that define the many water features, while also containing roof supports, lighting, and mechanical ductwork. The forms are representive of the rolling hills and mountains of the local landscape, or natural formations of water-sculpted stone. Pool users can move through the fantasy environment along a variety of water paths including slides, currents, and steps, with features such as waterfalls, whirlpools, waterjets, and caverns. A combination of skylights and artificial lighting enhance the extraordinary character of the space. > Taking advantage of the existing structures, the expansion preserves significant open and green spaces for sunbathing and other outdoor activities. To accomplish this, the architects adopted an L-shaped plan that incorporates a new family pool area extension, enclosing existing paved areas and pools. The building's entry faces the Ringstrasse, and emphasizes the linear arrival path with the addition of a wide, arching entry ramp to the south and an entry stair to the north. The sauna and fitness center extension are situated near the Ringstrasse so as not to encroach upon the lawn area. > Sauna facilities were planned to include both

SECTION THROUGH SAUNA WING, ENTRY COURTYARD, AND LOBBY   SECTION THROUGH NEW ENTRY AND EXISTING POOL

indoor and outdoor components, such as dry and steam saunas, cold dip pools, and relaxation lounges. The sauna bar provides food and drink service with access to a shared kitchen. A fitness center adjoins the sauna entry, housing tanning beds, massage rooms, and an exercise area with weight machines and cardiovascular machines such as stationary bikes, treadmills, and NordicTracks. > Support facilities, a café, and lifeguard areas are expanded and renovated to create a more linear flow pattern from entry to changing rooms, lockers, showers, toilets, and pools. Special changing rooms accommodate families, parents with infants, the handicapped, and individuals. A centrally located café has a counter with three service orientations, allowing efficient staffing from a single central food preparation area that is accessible from the main lobby, sauna, and outdoor areas. The relocated lifeguard area provides overview and emergency access to the existing pool, fantasy pool, and outdoor pool. > Renewable resource energy technologies will contribute to the thermal comfort of the building and pools. The roof of the fantasy pool tips up on the south side for direct solar heat gain, while the roof of the sauna slopes down to the south to provide surfaces for solar hot water collectors and photovoltaic cells. New access corridors for the changing rooms and fitness center are oriented to the southwest, collecting warm air and serving as thermal buffer zones. > The forms and materials of the renovation were influenced by the V shape of the existing pool roof. The folded plate geometries of the roofs combine to create an undulating roof line, which reinforces the nature-inspired forms of the fantasy pool. The new forms are envisioned with zinc roofs and a combination of clear glass, plaster, and translucent exterior walls.

135

LANDAU FILMS, SANTA MONICA, CALIFORNIA (1996)

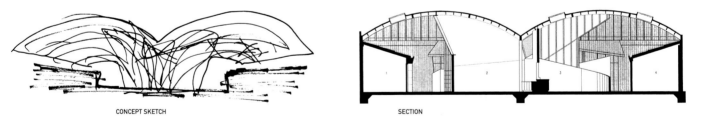

CONCEPT SKETCH

SECTION

LANDAU FILMS, SANTA MONICA, CALIFORNIA (1996) This interiors project for film production offices is located in the Broadway Gallery complex of Santa Monica, within a space that formerly housed the lithography studio of artist Sam Francis. > Art influences were significant in the evolution of the design. As the client is a collector and enthusiast, and the project is located inside the former Francis studio, the design acknowledged the artist and his contemporaries. Two of Francis' pieces informed the design concepts and use of color. *Blue Cut Sail, 1969* inspired the limited use of color on the perimeter walls. The resulting white center object and roof are free to be simultaneously understood as both everything and nothing; figural object and a neutral background. Within the main conference room the dominance of a central color is derived from *Five Stone Untitled, 1968*. > Other art pieces admired by the client and architect were referenced in the design process. The compression of space between the converging planes of the conference room entries are influenced by Richard Serra's *Running Arcs, 1992*. Another source, Franz Kline's paintings, with their undefined edges and strong visual movement, suggested spontaneity in the way the project's new interior forms responded to existing elements. Prompted by Jasper Johns' *1971 Voice 2*, the architect used the gray concrete floor to bind together the project's various colors and materials. Lastly, sculptures by Joel Shapiro are referenced because

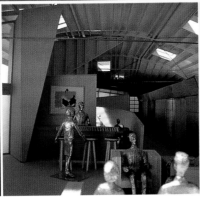

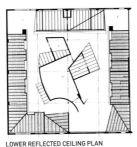
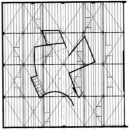

PLAN

LOWER REFLECTED CEILING PLAN

UPPER REFLECTED CEILING PLAN

TOP ROW, LEFT TO RIGHT:
Worm's eye view. Director's office.
Central conference room,
production pit, and film library.
Central conference room,
production pit, and staff kitchen.
SECOND ROW, LEFT TO RIGHT:
Sectional model. Director's office
interior. Client reception. Conference
room interior. Circulation area.

they share with the project a simple, kit-like assembly of pieces into meaningfully balanced compositions. > Existing brick walls, originally whitewashed as a neutral "canvas" to display Francis' art, combine with skylights, a painted wood ceiling, and steel cables to create a dramatic space. The program for the 6,400-square-foot (595-square-meter) project consists of a reception area and client space, offices, two conference rooms, a kitchen and café area, production pits, a tape library, and editing bays. > The design concepts dramatized the existing openness and raw character of the old warehouse. The 24-foot-high (7.3-meter-high) vaulted ceiling was too alluring to ignore and too powerful to challenge with a separate object. Perimeter office spaces are contained below the vaulted ceiling while the walls of the central spaces engage it, deflecting as necessary to encompass or avoid existing skylights. This central wall-object mediates the surrounding spaces, eliminating corridors in the conventional sense. These highly figural exposed frame walls extend up to the exposed wood roof framing so that walls and ceiling can be read as one, like a seagull with outspread wings. > Common or industrial materials used throughout the project include painted wood framing on the central object, drywall, plywood in the conference room interior, galvanized sheet metal on the perimeter office walls, polycarbonate panels on the perimeter office ceilings, and sealed concrete floors.

137

GROUND LEVEL PLAN

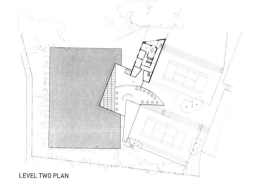

LEVEL TWO PLAN

SITE AND CONTEXT PLAN

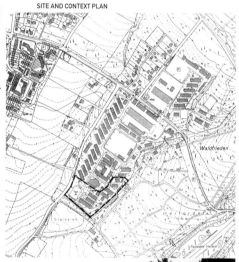

TENNIS CLUB HERFORD, HERFORD, GERMANY (1996) The Tennis Club Herford occupies a dense forest of hardwood trees near the town of Herford in Northern Germany. The site also contains foundations, pathways, and a few remaining buildings from a former British military barracks, which are evident within the existing parking layouts and tree clearings. > The vaulted forms of the new structure, clad in corrugated aluminum, recall the nearby remaining military buildings and history of the site, while evoking the visual movement and fluidity of tennis. The client's program consists of 11 outdoor courts, three indoor courts, a clubroom, a kitchen, a pro shop, locker rooms, and the manager's quarters. The enclosed spaces total 6,458 square feet (600 square meters). > Outdoor courts are oriented slightly to the west of the north-south axis to minimize the sun's impact on players' vision. Indoor courts are built on an existing foundation on a northwest-southeast axis. The remainder of the program occupies the wedge of space where the indoor and outdoor courts converge. This location influenced the concepts for the building, and the blank façades of the locker rooms and kitchen are used as the backdrop walls for the center court. Painted a dark green, the building's exterior engages the perimeter screens of the outdoor courts. > The center court consists of two courts with bleacher seating integrated into the natural terrain. A glass extension of the clubroom and a terrace for outdoor food and beverage service is situated between the two courts providing a variety of spaces for spectators. > The indoor courts are enclosed in a 45-foot-high (13.7-meter-high) vaulted form, supported by laminated wooden beams. Circulation areas are covered with an inverted vault, which tips up to create canopies for the main entry and the center court entry. > The building, fronting the forest, appears as a thin profile when viewed from the entry drive, parking, and entry sidewalks. End walls of all vaulted forms are clear glass. This transparency renders the building subordinate to the landscape, as the mature trees continue to dominate the experience of the site. From inside the complex, the sculptural aspect of the building composition becomes apparent.

ELEVATION

OPPOSITE, BOTTOM THREE IMAGES: Existing site conditions.
ABOVE, CLOCKWISE FROM TOP LEFT: Arial view of model. View into
enclosed courts. Arial view from parking. Building exterior and
center court. View across exterior courts. BELOW LEFT: Entry
view. BELOW RIGHT: Club café.

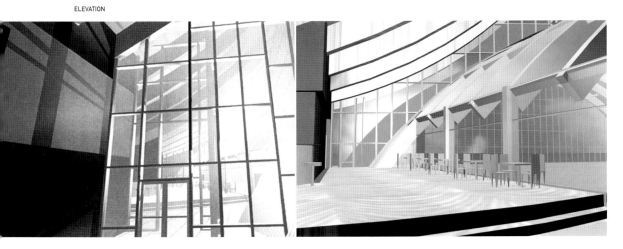

139

ART MUSEUM OF WESTERN VIRGINIA AND THE ADVANCE AUTO PARTS IMAX THEATER, ROANOKE, VIRGINIA (2006) ARCHITECT: Randall Stout Architects, Inc.: Randall Stout, FAIA, Principal-In-Charge PROJECT TEAM: Joel Cichowski, Robert Ley, Sandra Hutchings, Robert Arrand, Cynthia Bush, Jerry Chao, Danielle Lockareff, Jason Marshall, Steven A. Ruef, Kendall Walker, Hiroyuki Watanabe, Ann Yu AFFILIATE ARCHITECT: Rodriguez Ripley Maddux Motley: Benjamin Motley, AIA, Principal-In-Charge STRUCTURAL ENGINEER: John A. Martin & Associates, Inc. MECHANICAL ENGINEER: IBE Consulting Engineers, Inc. ELECTRICAL ENGINEER: Kocher & Schirra Consulting Engineers LANDSCAPE ARCHITECT: Whitsall Group CIVIL ENGINEER: Mattern & Craig COST ESTIMATOR: Lewicki Estimating Services CODE CONSULTANT: Rolf Jensen & Associates LIGHTING CONULTANT: Fisher Morantz Stone FOOD SERVICE CONSULTANT: Webb Design CONTRACTOR: TBD CLIENT: Art Museum of Western Virginia: Judy Larson, PhD., Executive Director; Bittle Porterfield, Chair, Board of Trustees and Building Committee

BALTIMORE MUSEUM OF ART, BALTIMORE, MARYLAND (2001) MUSEUM STRATEGIC PLANNING & PROGRAM CONSULTANT: M. Goodwin Associates, Inc.: Marcy Goodwin, Principal; Andrew Schuricht, Project Assistant SITE MASTER PLANNING AND MUSEUM SPACE PLANNING: Randall Stout Architects, Inc.: Randall Stout, Design Principal; Naina McKinley, Job Captain COST ESTIMATOR: Lewicki Estimating Services CODE CONSULTANT: Rolf Jensen & Associates CLIENT: Baltimore Museum of Art: Doreen Bolger, Director ; Alan Dirican, Deputy Director for Operations

BLAIR GRAPHICS, SANTA MONICA, CALIFORNIA (1999) ARCHITECT: Randall Stout Architects, Inc.: Randall Stout, FAIA, Principal-In-Charge: Brian Kutza, Job Captain PROJECT TEAM: B.J. Glidden, IV, Ann Yu STRUCTURAL ENGINEER: John A. Martin & Associates, Inc MECHANICAL ENGINEER: Rosenberg & Associates ELECTRICAL ENGINEER: Rosenberg & Associates CONTRACTOR: Sierra Pacific Constructors, Inc. CLIENT: Robert N. Blair

BÜCKEBURG GAS & WATER CO., BÜCKEBURG, GERMANY (1998) DESIGN ARCHITECT: Randall Stout Architects, Inc.: Randall Stout, FAIA, Principal-In-Charge PROJECT TEAM: Richard Claridge, Yukio Okeda, Timothy Williams EXECUTIVE ARCHITECT: UTEG GmbH: Hartwig Rullkötter, AKNW, Principal-In-Charge; Stefan Hoffmann, Project Manager PROJECT TEAM: Jürgen Beinke, Ralf Janke, Corinna Hokamp, Günter Bollert, Annemarie Capogrosso-Marx STRUCTURAL ENGINEER: Ing. Büro Harmening MECHANICAL ENGINEER: Ing. Büro Reimer ELECTRICAL ENGINEER: Ing. Büro Rutenkröger FRESCO ARTIST: Susanne Ludwig CLIENT: Stadtwerke Bückeburg GmbH

BLAIR RESIDENCE, DURANGO, COLORADO (2004) ARCHITECT: Randall Stout Architects, Inc.: Randall Stout, FAIA, Principal-In-Charge PROJECT TEAM: Sandra Hutchings, Jerry Chao STRUCTURAL ENGINEER: Reynolds, Eccher & Associates CONTRACTOR: Masterson Construction CLIENT: Robert and Tricia Blair.

BÜNDE FIRE STATION, BÜNDE, GERMANY (2001) DESIGN ARCHITECT: Randall Stout Architects, Inc.: Randall Stout, FAIA, Principal-In-Charge PROJECT TEAM: Jeffrey Garret, Sebastian Kaempf, Michael Pinto, Friedrich Tuczek EXECUTIVE ARCHITECT: Archimedes, GmbH, Bad Oeynhausen, Germany: Hartwig Rullkötter AKNW, Principal-In-Charge PROJECT TEAM: Günter Bollert, Stefan Hoffmann, Corinna Hokamp, Annemarie Capogrosso-Marx, Jürgen Beinke, Volker Barthelmes STRUCTURAL ENGINEER: Ing. Büro Diekmann MECHANICAL ENGINEER: Ing. Büro Reich + Hölscher ELECTRICAL ENGINEER: Ing. Büro Schröder CONTRACTOR: FA. Oberbremer CLIENT: Städt Bünde

COGNITO FILMS, CULVER CITY, CALIFORNIA (2002) ARCHITECT: Randall Stout Architects, Inc.: Randall Stout, FAIA, Principal-In-Charge Ann Yu, Job Captain PROJECT TEAM: Joel Cichowski, Naina McKinley, Danielle Lockareff STRUCTURAL ENGINEER: John A. Martin & Associates, Inc MECHANICAL & ELECTRICAL ENGINEER: Mazzetti & Associates CONTRACTOR: Crommie Construction Corporation CLIENT: Alan Landau

HUNTER MUSEUM OF AMERICAN ART, CHATTANOOGA, TENNESSEE (2005) ARCHITECT: Randall Stout Architects, Inc.: Randall Stout, FAIA, Principal-In-Charge; Sandra Hutchings, Project Designer; Rashmi Vasavada, Job Captain PROJECT TEAM: Cynthia Bush, Hailun Chang, Jerry Chao, Eric Cheong, Ian Collins, Amy Drezner, Robert Ley, Jason Marshall, Kendall Walker ASSOCIATE ARCHITECT: Derthick, Henley, & Wilkerson Architects: William Wilkerson, Principal-In-Charge; Andrew Roth, Ray Boaz COLLABORATING ARCHITECT, PROGRAMMING PHASE & URBAN DESIGN: Hefferlin + Kronenberg Architects PLLC: Heidi Hefferlin, Principal-In-Charge PROJECT TEAM: Emily Lingerfelt, Matt Culver, Brent Barron, James Williamson, Kimberly Stubbert, Elizabeth Davis STRUCTURAL ENGINEER: John A. Martin + Associates, Inc. MECHANICAL ENGINEER: March Adams Associates with IBE Consulting Engineers, Inc. ELECTRICAL ENGINEER: March Adams Associates LIGHTING CONSULTANT: Fisher Marantz Stone FOOD SERVICE CONSULTANT: Webb Design LANDSCAPE ARCHITECT: Ross/Fowler CIVIL ENGINEER: March

Adams Associates COST ESTIMATOR: Davis Langdon Adamson ACOUSTICS AND AUDIO/VIDEO: Newcomb & Boyd CURTAINWALL: CDC Curtainwall Consultants CONSTRUCTION MANAGER: EMJ Corporation CLIENT: Hunter Museum of American Art: Robert A. Kret, Director

LANDAU FILMS, SANTA MONICA, CALIFORNIA (1996) ARCHITECT: Randall Stout Architects, Inc.: Randall Stout, FAIA, Principal-In-Charge; Timothy Williams, Job Captain CLIENT: Alan Landau

MARION KOOGLER MCNAY ART MUSEUM, SAN ANTONIO, TEXAS (1997) MUSEUM STRATEGIC PLANNING & PROGRAM CONSULTANT: M. Goodwin Associates. Inc.: Marcy Goodwin, Principal; Julie Luckenbach, Project Assistant SITE MASTER PLANNING AND MUSEUM SPACE PLANNING: Randall Stout Architects, Inc.: Randall Stout, Design Principal PROJECT TEAM: Chip Minnick MEP CONSULTANT: Lester Rosenberg COST ESTIMATOR: Lewicki Estimating Services CLIENT: McNay Art Museum: Dr. William Chiego, Director

MATLIN RESIDENCE, VENICE, CALIFORNIA (2000) ARCHITECT: Randall Stout Architects, Inc.: Randall Stout, FAIA, Principal-In-Charge Ann Yu, Job Captain CLIENT: Olga Matlin

MELITTABAD AQUATICS FACILITY, MINDEN, GERMANY (1998) DESIGN ARCHITECT: Randall Stout Architects, Inc.: Randall Stout, FAIA, Principal-In-Charge PROJECT TEAM: Damien Bogert, Yukio Okeda EXECUTIVE ARCHITECT: UTEG GmbH with AGN UTEG TEAM: Hartwig Rullkötter, AKNW, Principal-In-Charge; Stefan Hoffmann, Project Manager PROJECT TEAM: Ralf Janke, Jürgen Beinke, Corinna Hokamp AGN TEAM: Christian Scharlau ENGINEER: Büro G. Reimer GmbH LANDSCAPE ARCHITECT: Mr. Oberbrauer CONCRETE CONSULTANT: Winterwerber & Partner LIGHTING CONSULTANT: Mr. Braun CONTRACTOR: Paul Niederberghaus & Partner CLIENT: Mindener Bäder GmbH, Stadtwerke Minden

MONTCLAIR POLICE STATION, MONTCLAIR, CALIFORNIA (2005) ARCHITECT: Randall Stout Architects, Inc.: Randall Stout, FAIA, Principal-In-Charge; Steven A. Ruef, Project Director PROJECT TEAM: Cynthia Bush, Sandra Hutchings, Jerry Chao, Hiroyuki Watanabe STRUCTURAL ENGINEER: John A. Martin & Associates COST ESTIMATOR: Davis Langdon Adamson CLIENT: City of Montclair: Lee McDougal, City Manager; Chief Chester Thompson, Chief of Police; Lt. Keith Jones, Project Manager

NORTH CAROLINA MUSEUM OF ART, RALEIGH, NORTH CAROLINA (1997) MUSEUM STRATEGIC PLANNING & PROGRAM CONSULTANT: M. Goodwin Associates. Inc.: Marcy Goodwin, Principal SITE MASTER PLANNING AND MUSEUM SPACE PLANNING: Randall Stout Architects, Inc.:; Randall Stout, Design Principal; Timothy Williams, Job Captain COST ESTIMATOR: Lewicki Estimating Services CLIENT: North Carolina Museum of Art: Dr. Lawrence Wheeler, Director; Daniel Gottleib, Project Manager

NORTH MINDEN POWER PLANT, MINDEN, GERMANY (1996) DESIGN ARCHITECT: Randall Stout Architects, Inc.: Randall Stout, FAIA, Principal-In-Charge DESIGN TEAM: Damien Bogert, Yukio Okeda EXECUTIVE ARCHITECT: UTEG GmbH: Hartwig Rullkötter, AKNW, Principal-In-Charge PROJECT TEAM: Friedhelm Diekmann, Ralf Janke, Stefan Hoffmann, Simone Weithöner, Günter Bollert, Corinna Hokamp, Annemarie Capogrosso-Marx ENGINEERS: Büro G. Reimer GmbH STRUCTURAL ENGINEER: Büro Moller POWER PRODUCTION TECHNOLOGY CONSULTANTS: Andreas Huck, Jürgen Ehrenreich GENERAL CONTRACTOR: Haack + Klauke + Schlüter (Construction Manager) CLIENT: ARGE Fernwärme, a cooperative project of Stadtwerke Minden and Elektrizitätswerk Minden-Ravensberg GmbH: Dr. Manfred Ragati, IUR, EMR Director

POST OAK CENTRAL, HOUSTON, TEXAS (1989) DESIGN: Randall Stout, FAIA ADVISORS: Albert Pope, O. Jack Mitchell CRITICS: Peter Waldman, Richard Ingersoll

REHME WATER STATION, REHME, GERMANY (2000) DESIGN ARCHITECT: Randall Stout Architects, Inc.: Randall Stout, FAIA, Principal-In-Charge DESIGN TEAM: Wes Adachi, Richard Claridge, Robert Hsin, Chip Minnick EXECUTIVE ARCHITECT: Archimedes GmbH: Hartwig Rullkötter, AKNW, Principal-In-Charge PROJECT TEAM: Stefan Hoffmann, Günter Bollert, Corinna Hokamp, Annemarie Capogrosso-Marx STRUCTURAL ENGINEER: Ing. Büro Schöne TECHNICAL ENGINEER: KLT Consult CONTRACTOR: A.F. Groh CLIENT: Städtische Wasserwerk Bad Oeynhausen

RHODE ISLAND SCHOOL OF DESIGN MUSEUM, PROVIDENCE, RHODE ISLAND (1999) MUSEUM STRATEGIC PLANNING & PROGRAM CONSULTANT: M. Goodwin Associates. Inc.: Marcy Goodwin, Principal; Julie Luckenbach, Project Assistant SITE MASTER PLANNING AND MUSEUM SPACE PLANNING: Randall Stout Architects, Inc.: Randall Stout, Design Principal; Ann Yu, Job Captain COST ESTIMATOR: Lewicki Estimating Services CLIENT: Rhode Island School of Design, Museum of Art: Phillip M. Johnston, Director

SEATTLE ART MUSEUM, SEATTLE, WASHINGTON (1999) MUSEUM STRATEGIC PLANNING & PROGRAM CONSULTANT: M. Goodwin Associates. Inc.: Marcy Goodwin, Principal; Julie Luckenbach, Project Assistant SITE MASTER PLANNING AND MUSEUM SPACE PLANNING: Randall Stout Architects, Inc.: Randall Stout, Design Principal; Ann Yu, Job Captain COST ESTIMATOR: Lewicki Estimating Services CLIENT: Seattle Art Museum: Mimi Gates, Director; Gail Joice, Associate Director; Jeff Eby, Chief Financial Officer

SIMEONSPLATZ, MINDEN, GERMANY (1996) DESIGN ARCHITECT: Randall Stout Architects. Inc.: Randall Stout, FAIA, Principal-In-Charge PROJECT TEAM: Damien Bogert, Yukio Okeda LOCAL ARCHITECTS: UTEG GmbH and Büro Parallel LOCAL ARCHITECT TEAM: Hartwig Rullkötter, AKNW, Principal-In-Charge PROJECT TEAM: Simone Weithöner, Annemarie Capogrosso-Marx CLIENT: City of Minden

STEINHÜDE SEA RECREATIONAL FACILITY, STEINHÜDE, GERMANY (2000) DESIGN ARCHITECT: Randall Stout Architects, Inc.: Randall Stout, FAIA, Principal-In-Charge PROJECT TEAM: Friedrich Tuczek, Timothy Williams, Wes Adachi, Richard Claridge, Sebastian Kaempf, Stephanie Kaindl, Yukio Okeda EXECUTIVE ARCHITECT: Archimedes GmbH: Hartwig Rullkötter, AKNW, Principal-In-Charge; Stefan Hoffmann, Project Manager PROJECT TEAM: Jürgen Beinke, Corinna Hohkamp STRUCTURAL ENGINEER: IHV Objektbau Dipl.-Ing. Hubert Wemheuer, Prüfingenieur für Baustatik ENERGY ADVISOR: Jürgen Kötter MECHANICAL ENGINEER: IHV Objektbau ELECTRICAL ENGINEER: IHV Objektbau CONTRACTOR: IHV Objektbau CLIENT: Elektrizitätswerk Minden-Ravensberg GmbH

SUPERCOLLIDER CITY, CENTRAL TEXAS (1988) DESIGN: Randall Stout, FAIA ADVISOR: Danny Samuels CRITICS: Albert Pope, Peter Waldman, Lars Lerup

TELEOS TELECOM HEADQUARTERS, KIRCHLENGERN, GERMANY (1998) DESIGN ARCHITECT: Randall Stout Architects, Inc.: Randall Stout, FAIA, Principal-In-Charge PROJECT TEAM: Sebastian Keampf, Stephanie Kaindl, Friedrich Tuczek EXECUTIVE ARCHITECT: Archimedes GmbH: Hartwig Rullkötter, AKNW, Principal-In-Charge CLIENT: Telios Telecommunications Group: Dr. Manfred Ragati, IUR

TENNIS CLUB HERFORD, HERFORD, GERMANY (1996) DESIGN ARCHITECT: Randall Stout Architects, Inc.: Randall Stout, FAIA, Principal-In-Charge PROJECT TEAM: Timothy Williams, Damien Bogert, Yukio Okeda EXECUTIVE ARCHITECT: UTEG GmbH: Hartwig Rullkötter, AKNW, Principal-In-Charge CLIENT: Tennis Club Herford

UNIVERSITY OF CALIFORNIA, RIVERSIDE, ALUMNI AND VISITORS CENTER, RIVERSIDE, CALIFORNIA (2005) ARCHITECT: Randall Stout Architects, Inc.: Randall Stout, FAIA, Principal-In-Charge; Ann Yu, Job Captain PROJECT TEAM: Joel Cichowski, Robert Arrand, Danielle Lockareff, Kendall Walker STRUCTURAL ENGINEER: John A. Martin & Associates, Inc MECHANICAL AND ELECTRICAL ENGINEERS: Gilmore & Associates/Rosenberg & Associates COST ESTIMATOR: Davis Langdon Adamson FOOD SERVICE CONSULTANT: Webb Design CONTRACTOR: TBD CLIENT: University of California, Riverside: Dan Johnson, Director Design and Construction; Darius Maroufkhani, Project Manager; Kyle Hoffman, Assistant Vice Chancellor Alumni & Constituent Relations; Dave Willmon, Immediate Past President Alumni Association

VIRGINIA MUSEUM OF FINE ARTS, RICHMOND, VIRGINIA (1998) MUSEUM STRATEGIC PLANNING & PROGRAM CONSULTANT: M. Goodwin Associates. Inc.: Marcy Goodwin, Principal SITE MASTER PLANNING AND MUSEUM SPACE PLANNING: Randall Stout Architects, Inc.: Randall Stout, Design Principal; B.J. Glidden IV, Job Captain COST ESTIMATOR: Lewicki Estimating Services CLIENT: Virginia Museum of Fine Arts: Dr. Katharine Lee, Director; Richard Woodward, Associate Director/Project Manager

WASSON RESIDENCE, NORRIS, TENNESSEE (2004) ARCHITECT: Randall Stout Architects, Inc.: Randall Stout, FAIA, Principal-In-Charge; Danielle Lockareff, Job Captain PROJECT TEAM: Ann Yu, Robert Ley, Jason Marshall, Hiroyuki Watanabe, Robert Arrand STRUCTURAL ENGINEER: Bender & Associates GENERAL CONTRACTOR: Rodney Braden CLIENT: Michael and Marcia Wasson

WESTGATE MEDIA PARK, LOS ANGELES, CALIFORNIA (2002) ARCHITECT: Randall Stout Architects, Inc.: Randall Stout, FAIA, Principal-In-Charge; Robert Arrand, Job Captain PROJECT TEAM: Jerry Chao, Danielle Lockareff, Rashmi Vasavada, Ann Yu STRUCTURAL ENGINEER: Brandow & Johnston ELECTRICAL ENGINEER: Mazzetti & Associates CONTRACTOR: Tarantino Construction, Inc. CLIENT: Westgate LaGrange Partners, LTD.: Michael Schuminsky

PHOTOGRAPHY CREDITS:
RSA: Jerry Chao: page 122 (bottom four images); Peter Hübbe: cover & pages 12-15, 26-36, 38-43, 44 (top right), 45-48, 49 (top, bottom left, & middle), 56-67, 68 (top & bottom left), 69-71, 73 (top right), 74-75; RSA: Sebastian Kaempf: page 132 (bottom two images), 133; Landiscor Aerial Information: page 95 (top); David Adamson, Lone Pine Pictures: pages 24, 25 (right). Randall Stout: pages 16-17, 25 (left), 37, 44 (top left), 49 (bottom right), 52 (bottom left), 68 (bottom right), 72, 73 (top left), 76-77, 83-89, 91-93, 97-121, 122 (top), 124-131, 132 (top four & middle three images), 134-139; Joshua White: pages 18-23, 50-51, 52 (bottom middle & right), 53-55.

ACKNOWLEDGMENTS BY RANDALL STOUT

Over the years so many have supported my architectural explorations, it is difficult to acknowledge everyone, but there are those who have had a lasting impact on my career and life. It gives me great pleasure to extend these personal thanks.

> Great appreciation is hereby expressed to those who were especially influential and encouraging during my architectural education and development: Architects Dan Brewer, David Denton, James Glymph, Robert Hale, Kirk Hamilton, Craig Hartman, Randy Jefferson, Richard Keating, and Walter Netsch; and Professors Alton Delong, L. Duane Grieve, Richard Ingersoll, Albert Pope, William Shell, and Peter Waldman. To Frank Gehry I extend special thanks for allowing me to participate for so long in his creative process; for teaching by example how to be truly observant of the physical environment; and for showing how to engage emotive experiences during the design process.

> I also thank those who have generously supported the work through discussions, writings, and collegial or academic relationships: Jasper Cornett, Marleen Davis, Mark Dillon, James Franklin, Michael Garrison, Joseph Giovannini, Richard Gowe, Ann Gray, David Lawrence Gray, Don Griffith, David Hay, Michael Hricak, Laura Hull, Robert Ivy, Rob Jernigan, Stephan Kanner, Elizabeth Harrison Kubany, Reed Kroloff, Sylvia Lavin, Mark Lee, Greg Lynn, Liz Martin, David Meckel, Kara Mullio, Morris Newman, Danette Riddle, Vincent Snyder, Vance Travis, Ann Videriksen, Gregory Walsh, Michael Webb, and Bernard Zimmerman.

> I thank the trustees and the administrative leaders at the museums where I have consulted. They brought a clear understanding of their respective institutions and the role of the museum in the community, which contributed greatly to the planning vision. I especially thank Directors Georgianne Bingham, Dr. Doreen Bolger, Dr. William Chiego, Mimi Gates, Phillip Johnston, Robert Kret, Dr. Judy Larson, Katharine Lee Reid, and Dr. Lawrence Wheeler; Associate Directors Gail Joice and Richard Woodward; and Project Directors Alan Dirican, Jeff Eby, and Daniel Gottlieb.

> I sincerely thank the many colleagues and consultants listed in the credits and recognize their contributions to the work, especially those with whom our extended affiliation has produced numerous successful projects and lasting friendships. These include Marcy Goodwin, M. Goodwin & Associates; Dr. Manfred Ragati, Hartwig Rullkötter, and Jurgen Kötter, UTEG/Archimedes; and Trailer Martin and Chuck Whitaker, John A. Martin & Associates.

> The works shown in this publication are not created in isolation; rather they require the dedication of talented collaborators. The many staff members, as indicated in the project credits, are appreciated for their skillful and enthusiastic participation. I extend special recognition and thanks to Associates Sandra Hutchings, Yukio Okeda, Timothy Williams, and Ann G. Yu, whose lasting contributions have been an integral part of the firm's success and recognition.

> Several people worked tirelessly to provide the organization, graphics, and text of this monograph: special thanks to Kendall Walker, Cynthia Bush, Sandra Hutchings, and Marcy Goodwin for all their efforts. I would also like to extend my many thanks to Anthony Iannacci and Sarah Palmer at Edizioni for their endless patience and constant support in the compilation of this monograph. And lastly my sincere appreciation to Joseph Giovannini for his time and energy spent visiting the studio and delving into my work to introduce this monograph with insight and clarity.

> I am especially indebted to my early clients, Dr. Manfred Ragati, Robert Blair, Alan Landau, Michael Schuminsky, and the University of California, Riverside, for seeing the potential of my practice and for courageously forging new architectural territory. Thank you for your trust, foresight, and contributions to our design process.

> Lastly, I would like to thank my family. To my parents Roger and Gloria Stout, thanks for the high value placed on knowledge, discovery, education, respect for nature, and for instilling a desire to better peoples lives. The consistent encouragement, unwavering support, belief, and love exhibited throughout my education and practice by my parents, grandparents C.E. and Ruth Stout and E.W. and Marie Mynatt, and siblings, Steve Stout and Marcia Stout Wasson, is most appreciated. To my wife Joelle Stout, thanks for sharing your boundless love and enduring faith. You have brought great joy to my life, including our sons Colton and Logan.

143